Praise for *12 Months to $1 Million*

"Ryan has been on my podcast several times, and I enjoy watching his journey. As douchey as this title is, I am confident that it will inspire a new kind of entrepreneur."

—**Gary Vaynerchuk,** chairman of VaynerX and bestselling author

"I failed as an entrepreneur countless times before the idea for Poo~Pourri came to me when I was 42. My first year of business I exceeded $1 million in sales, and I couldn't have done it without the lessons I learned from all my prior businesses. I wholeheartedly believe those experiences are a necessary part of success, and Ryan has used his own challenges—and the knowledge of so many inspiring and successful entrepreneurs that came before us—to outline a recipe that will make it so much easier to expand your business and yourself. Pay attention and reap the benefits!"

—**Suzy Batiz,** creator and CEO of Poo~Pourri and supernatural

"Ryan is literally the person that I reached out to when I decided to start a business. I've met and interacted with his students, and his success stories are too many to name. His events are top of class, especially when I'm the emcee. With the world as polarized as it is, it takes a special ability to present a unifying message around business, money, and capitalism, and Ryan does just that. I've never seen someone provide such a detailed playbook to hitting your first million, and there is no one better to do this than Ryan Daniel Moran."

—**JP Sears,** comedian, author, and host of *Awaken With JP*

Case Studies

"Ryan's strategies and education were an integral part to helping us grow our business past the million mark within the first year. After crossing seven figures, we continued to work with Ryan as we scaled from seven figures to eight. After two and a half years of running our business, we were fortunate to have an eight-figure exit. Today, we have the freedom to travel the world and invest in exciting projects. To say that this formula has changed my life would be a huge understatement."

—**Alex Upperman,** Kansas City, MO

"Thanks to Ryan's videos, podcasts, and live events, I am on pace to have a seven-figure business this year—that's a big number for an immigrant from Ukraine! However, Ryan's work has helped me see that the payoff is more than financial. I've created a community under my brand, Travelization. I realize now that my business can help me make a positive change. Personal wealth happens automatically when you create unique value for others. This is such a fun game—it has given me financial freedom and the ability to impact people around the world."

—**Andri Sadlak,** Vancouver, BC

"Today, I not only run my own business, but I also advise and speak on stages about this business. None of this would have ever happened if I hadn't been open to starting something completely new. I worked hard—and I still do—but now I have the freedom to call my own shots for life. I can directly track my new life to the day that I discovered Ryan's work. No matter where you are on your journey, pay attention—this is a wild ride!"

—**Yev Marusenko,** Seattle, WA

"I was thirty-eight when I started my first product's brand. I only dreamed of having the success that it would have—with over $100 million in sales the first year, hundreds of jobs created, and millions of customers affected around the world. I wish this book had existed when I began my journey, as it contains many critical tips and lessons I had to learn the hard way. It is a must-read for every aspiring entrepreneur. Strap in—you're in for a heck of an adventure."

—**Josh Bezoni,** BioTrust, Austin, TX

"This material quite literally helped make me a millionaire. If you're an aspiring entrepreneur and want the chance to ditch the traditional 'work 40–50 years in a 9 to 5 job and then retire when you're old' path, you should follow the formula that Ryan laid out and people like me have implemented and changed our lives with."

—**Chad Maghielse,** Grand Rapids, Michigan/Luquillo, Puerto Rico

"Ryan and his methods helped me grow TruDog into the 39th fastest privately held company in America. Right before we got our dream exit, our stock was valued at $100 million! If Ryan can start with nothing and build something—well so can I! Thank you, Ryan, for always being an inspiration."

—**Lori Taylor,** Cincinatti, OH

"When someone claims to have a formula to make millions, it's easy to be skeptical. However, since we had heard so many great things about Ryan, my husband and I took a chance on a workshop a year after starting our business—and I'm so glad we did. Not only did we walk away with tangible strategies to implement immediately, but, most important, Ryan inspired us to THINK BIG. Two years later we sold our first company for eight figures, and I couldn't be more excited about the future."

—**Shauna Chadwell,** Kansas City, MO

"From a job in corporate America ten years ago to starting an online insurance agency, I always had a hunger for more. Today, I run several seven-figure online businesses and a marketing agency and travel the world to give speeches to other entrepreneurs. However, what excites me most is that the freedom I now experience has allowed me to become a better husband, father, and friend. Ryan's content and the clarity that he provides has been a big part of my growth."

—**Liran Hirschkorn,** Long Island, NY

"My husband and I always dreamed of starting a nonprofit when we retired from our medical practice. We always thought that it would be a twenty-year project, but that all changed when we heard Ryan Daniel Moran give the '12 Months to $1 Million' presentation for the first time. Not only has our business gone from nothing to the mid-seven figures in just a few years, but we sold our medical practice so that we can start our nonprofit more than a decade earlier than we thought. Starting this business has been the craziest, most fun, most challenging, and most rewarding thing that my husband and I have ever done (besides having kids!)."

—**Jenna Zigler,** Austin, TX

"I became an entrepreneur because I wanted freedom. I knew that I was made for something more than sitting at a desk all day. Ryan's work gave me the playbook for turning my dream into a reality. I crossed seven figures after my first year, and three years in, I sold my business for a payday that set my family and me up for life. This journey isn't easy, but it's worth it; not only for the financial possibilities, but because of the person you become along the way."

—**Chris Nowak,** Dallas, TX

"I always dreamed of having freedom from a job and living life how I wanted, but I never had a clear plan to make it happen. When I heard Ryan's '12 Months to $1 Million' plan at a live event, everything changed. It gave me a roadmap to follow to grow my business, and we crossed the seven-figure mark within about two years. Today, my wife, Katie, and I both get to work within the business full-time. Being an entrepreneur isn't easy—it takes a lot of dedication and focus—but Ryan's podcasts and videos have always helped me when I needed an extra push. My advice to new entrepreneurs is to 'go for it,' because this plan works."

—**Devin Dorosh,** St. Louis, MO

"Since discovering the '12 Months To $1 Million' plan, I have proudly built my first internet business beyond the seven-figure mark. It has allowed me to be a full-time entrepreneur and to live life on my own terms. I work hard, I believe in what we are creating, and I am passionate about growing every day. Everything started with this playbook and my desire to succeed."

—**Justin Ray,** Fort Collins, CO

"As of this past year, I am proud to say that our business crossed seven figures; the '12 Months To $1 Million' plans works, and I am proof of it! I love being a full-time entrepreneur and am so proud of what we are building."

—**Jason Franciosa,** Element 26

"This book has lots of words in it, and I like that. Also, I really like the size of the book. I can't read yet, but I'm sure other people will like it."

—**Esther Moran,** 4 Years Old

12 MONTHS
—— TO ——
$1 MILLION

How to Pick a Winning Product,
Build a Real Business, and Become a
SEVEN-FIGURE ENTREPRENEUR

RYAN DANIEL MORAN

BenBella Books, Inc.
Dallas, TX

12 Months to $1 Million copyright © 2020 by Ryan Moran

BenBella

BenBella Books, Inc.
10440 N. Central Expressway, Suite 800
Dallas, TX 75231
www.benbellabooks.com
Send feedback to feedback@benbellabooks.com

BenBella is a federally registered trademark.

Printed in the United States of America
10 9 8 7 6 5 4 3 2 1

Library of Congress Control Number: 2019051641
ISBN 9781948836951 (print)
ISBN 9781950665143 (electronic)

Editing by Gregory Brown
Copyediting by Elizabeth Degenhard
Cover design by 99designs/TopHills and Sarah Avinger
Text design by Publishers' Design & Production Services, Inc.
Composition by PerfecType, Nashville, TN
Proofreading by Christine Florie and Michael Fedison
Indexing by WordCo Indexing Services, Inc.
Printed by Lake Book Manufacturing

Distributed to the trade by Two Rivers Distribution, an Ingram brand
www.tworiversdistribution.com

Special discounts for bulk sales are available. Please contact bulkorders@benbellabooks.com.

For Esther.
You were born for such a time as this.
Love,
Dad

NOTE

All examples, podcast interviews, and case studies can be downloaded for free at www.Capitalism.com/best.

CONTENTS

FOREWORD

"You're one funnel away."

These words are my promise to entrepreneurs.

My name is Russell Brunson, and I lead a community of entrepreneurs who build simple and profitable businesses. We call ourselves "funnel hackers."

I have personally seen thousands of women and men create businesses with nothing more than an idea and a drive to succeed. To date, we have more than 600 community members in our "two-comma club"—individuals who sold at least a million dollars on our software platform, ClickFunnels.

None of us come with silver spoons in our mouths. We don't have big teams, and we don't cheat by raising money from venture capital firms; if anyone does invest in us, it is usually a few thousand dollars from someone who believed in our crazy dreams. We don't begin with unique skills or previous experience. We don't come from families of business moguls. We are simply passionate business builders who can't do anything *except* be entrepreneurs.

Why? Because above else, *we desire freedom.*

We desire the freedom to give more to our families, our communities, and our churches, and we desire to leave the world better than how we found it. We desire the freedom to give our kids the advantages that we did not have. We desire the freedom to see the world and live life on our own terms.

I believe that every person is one funnel, one idea, or one breakthrough away from their version of freedom. You are one funnel away from the life that you want. One funnel away from a seven-figure business (if you want it to grow that big). One funnel away from the life that you desire most.

There are thousands of us, and we are changing the world.

As successful as we may be, our family of "funnel hackers" is just one drop in the wave of entrepreneurship that started blossoming after 2008. Until then, entrepreneurship was risky; who wants to take a risk when you can have a cozy, cushy job?

But once the idea of a safe and secure career came crashing down with the economy, dreamers like us decided that we might as well take a shot at creating life on our own terms. If it was possible to lose everything in an economic collapse, then we might as well take a small risk to be happy and free for the rest of our lives!

That was when pioneers in our industry started breaking the mold. Entrepreneurs who had been sitting on the sidelines started to find ways around the system, and together, we broke all the rules of business.

As a result, the floodgates of opportunity blew wide open. People who had never owned a business before started getting into the game.

Opportunities like social media, crowdfunding, Amazon, funnel hacking, drop shipping, and other new technologies made it possible for anyone to start a business. Even the "average" person could create a product (or sell someone else's) and become a full-time entrepreneur.

Some people became millionaires. And it continues to happen every single day.

While entrepreneurship used to be weird, it is now a popular and desired career. Kids across the world want to grow up to be entrepreneurs. That's a good thing because we are the ones who create jobs, create opportunity, and (as Ryan likes to put it) create change.

We are still in the second inning of this wave of entrepreneurship. More and more opportunities will open up over the coming years, and everyone with the desire for freedom should pay attention now.

New entrepreneurs are being created every day. Some of them start fun side hustles, while others go full-time, and many hit seven or eight figures. No matter how big your ambitions, there has never been more opportunity than today.

For those of us who *must* have freedom and *are called* to be entrepreneurs, this is the most exciting time in history to be alive.

That is why I am so excited about this book.

About once a decade, a book comes along that sparks new ideas for dreamers like us. That book throws open the doors for entrepreneurs, and it encourages dreamers to get off the sidelines and begin their quest for freedom. In the past, books like *Rich Dad Poor Dad* by Robert Kiyosaki, *The 4-Hour Work Week* by Tim Ferriss, and *Crush It!* by Gary Vaynerchuk inspired a new generation of business owners; these books are considered classics because they continue to inspire entrepreneurs to this day.

I believe that the book you are reading right now—*12 Months to $1 Million* by Ryan Daniel Moran—is the next classic for this generation of entrepreneurs. His simple yet wildly effective formula to hit seven figures has set hundreds of entrepreneurs free to create exciting businesses.

I first discovered Ryan Daniel Moran when I saw his now-famous t-shirt in a viral video on Facebook. It read:

~~Democrat~~

~~Republican~~

ENTREPRENEUR

Right away, I knew that he was someone who thought differently. This was someone who wasn't afraid to resist the norms and push the limits of what was normal.

However, I didn't meet Ryan in person until he asked me to speak at his event, the Capitalism Conference. At first I declined, but then Ryan made me an offer I could not refuse: He offered to have a private jet pick me up in Boise, fly me through the night to Austin, Texas, and then have me home in time for dinner with my family.

This guy knows how to get things done, I thought.

As impressed as I was, the community of entrepreneurs at his event impressed me even more. Men and women had flown from all over the world to grow their businesses. Many of them had become millionaires in two years or less. All of them were eager to learn, excited to grow, and passionate to do more in the world.

This was more than a "rah-rah" event full of slimy salespeople. Instead, this community was giving, present, and eager to make a difference. They were true capitalists: people who take ownership for their lives, create value, and serve their community.

I am honored to support and endorse anyone who can raise a community like that.

Like myself, Ryan grew up with very few opportunities, but a lot of big dreams. He figured out this game in the trenches. People like us didn't grow up with "how-to" manuals, so it's our responsibility to empower the next generation of entrepreneurs with the knowledge that we learned along the way.

I do that through my books, my podcast, and my yearly event, Funnel Hacking Live. Ryan has been doing it for years through his podcast, but nothing compares to the book that you hold in your hands.

When I discovered Ryan's podcast a few years ago, I discovered someone who was willing to share *everything*. He shared the exact strategies to pick the right products, get them selling profitably, and how to grow a seven-figure business that you can ultimately sell if you want to. He also shared how he invested money so that he would be free for life.

Ryan is one of the rare characters on the internet who willingly shares everything. More than that, he shares the ups and downs, which few are willing to do. Instead of flashing fancy cars or claiming that everything is fine and well, Ryan opens up about challenges in a way that helps entrepreneurs overcome their own struggles and move forward with more confidence. My favorite video that he ever did is called, "All I Ever Wanted to Be Was a Millionaire" (if you have never seen it, it is worth a Google).

I also discovered that Ryan's strategies complemented mine perfectly. While I help people build cash-positive businesses that produce amazing short-term results, Ryan focuses on building long-term assets that can be scaled or even sold.

I do not always agree with his opinions, and he certainly is willing to be more controversial than me, but the results of his students speak for themselves. Between the two of us, it might be argued that we have helped to create more millionaires than any duo in history.

This is the single greatest time in history to be an entrepreneur. This is the best time ever to live a life of freedom. Before now, men and women did not have access to this knowledge. Entrepreneurs had to figure it out on their own.

This book is a roadmap to building a million-dollar business. That may seem impossible right now, but I have seen it happen thousands of times. I have met Ryan's students, and I have seen their success. They think big. They work hard. They do things differently. They are ahead of the curve. And most importantly, they follow the formula in this book, because it works.

Never in my career have I seen so many entrepreneurs building *real* businesses that will be around for years to come. This book is the manual to making it happen.

I am confident that the entrepreneurs who read this book will be well equipped to build exciting businesses that make a positive impact in the world.

I am proud to have been featured onstage at Ryan's events and on his podcast. I am proud to have Ryan in my "two-comma club." Most of all, I am proud and excited to give my endorsement for the book that you hold in your hands; this is a life-changing moment for you and the thousands of people that you will impact with your success.

You are a funnel away. You are one idea away. You are one product away. You are one moment away.

While you read this book, the ideas will come to life in your mind. You will imagine yourself doing this, and you will clearly see your business in your mind.

There are thousands of entrepreneurs who have come before you who have blazed this trail. We are cheering for you, and we are counting on you. You're a capitalist, and the world is counting on you.

God bless.

Russell Brunson
Founder, ClickFunnels.com

Don't Read This Book

If you picked up this book because you're intrigued by the short-term goal of making a million dollars in twelve months, let me start by quoting Dan Sullivan: "Being an entrepreneur is a life sentence."

Actually, it's more like an epic adventure—but it does last a lifetime. It's not a tale of orderly and sequential wins. It's a long and uneven road peppered with heartbreaking losses, crippling self-doubt, episodes of depression, and the heaviness of carrying everything on one's shoulders.

Like any adventure, though, there's something truly valuable at the end of that road. After facing challenges you couldn't have anticipated or prepared for, there's victory. There's freedom. There's the ability to call your own shots. And, most importantly, there's a new hero at the end of the adventure: you.

There is no game more challenging and rewarding than entrepreneurship. Once you get the itch, it never really gets fully scratched. Once you get the first taste, you never turn back. It will be that way for life. Once you are called to be an entrepreneur, there's simply no other satisfying way you can spend your days.

Starting a business requires more sacrifice than I ever imagined. So, why do I do it? Simple: because there's nothing else I can do *and* be happy doing.

If this sounds like you—if freedom is your calling, and you *have* to have it—then consider this book the roadmap for your adventure. In these pages you'll learn how to become a seven-figure entrepreneur. This plan is proven to work. Hundreds of success stories have come before you, making your path easier.

Entrepreneurs are weird. We are few. We see things differently. The rest of the world debates us, judges us, and even sometimes blames us for achieving success. But we create change, and the world needs more people like us.

If you're one of the weird ones, then this is your invitation to answer the call.

If you're not? Then please *don't* turn the page.

Believe me, I'm not saying this to try to create false intrigue—I'm dead serious. This is a *warning*, not a sales pitch. This book's roadmap is so effective it can turn even the moderately curious—the window-shoppers, if you will—into successful entrepreneurs. If you casually go down this road, and you commit to the plan within these pages, you may very well find yourself quickly responsible for a million-dollar business. I don't use the word "responsible" lightly. I wouldn't wish entrepreneurship on anyone who's not cut out for it or dedicated to the amount of work it takes.

This roadmap is for the entrepreneurs who have been searching, seeking, and grinding their way to success. It has worked for single moms who desperately needed a change. It has worked for bankrupt families who needed new hope. It has worked for young kids who wanted to do something different with their lives. You will meet many such success stories in the pages of this book. With hope, you'll see yourself in their tales.

But this method can also cause challenges for those who aren't ready for the blood, sweat, and tears it requires. Starting a business without the right mindset will consume your days, destroy your work-life balance, and make you question what the hell you're doing on a moment-to-moment basis. You'll doubt yourself in ways you didn't know possible.

In fact, I recently heard billionaire Dan Pena say he would *never* do it all over again. The pursuit becomes all-consuming and never really ends. Plus, he said, there were too many missed days with his children.

You have the chance here to simply close this book and walk away. Or, hey—give it to that friend you know who has masochistic tendencies (we've all got a friend like that, right?). If you're happy with your life, keep living it how it is. Wake up in your bed tomorrow, enjoy your breakfast, and be thankful there are crazy people in the world who will give up everything to bleed over their businesses in pursuit of success.

But if you *know*—if you're 100 percent *certain*—that you're one of those crazy people . . . strap in.

By turning the page, you're committing to the process of building something great. If you follow this roadmap, there's a good chance that you will have a million-dollar business one year from now. This is your epic adventure, and your journey begins now.

INTRODUCTION

When I was a kid, I asked my dad how much a million dollars was. My dad was a middle school teacher for more than thirty years. He gave his life to his profession to provide for his kids and to create a retirement. As a teacher, he never had much chance of being a millionaire.

"Ryan," he said, "if I worked for my entire career, and *never* spent any of the money I ever made, then I would have about a million dollars."

It took me a few years to process that. But if you run the numbers, it makes sense. Once you factor in taxes, teachers tend to take home an average of about $40,000 a year. To make a million dollars, they'd have to work for twenty-five years, *and never spend a dime.*

Jeez.

I decided then and there that I wanted to become a millionaire. I don't know why; perhaps I equated being a millionaire with being free. I mean, hell, a million bucks invested at just 6 percent interest would bring in the same annual income my dad earned for the rest of my life. I'd be able to do whatever I wanted (ignore, for the moment, the adorably naïve kid-think that $40k a year equals doing whatever one wants).

At the time, I was just a business-minded kid with no idea what the runway to becoming a millionaire was like. After reading up on some obvious ways of making money—real estate, the stock market—I realized these paths seemed long, slow, and pretty dull. I didn't like the lack of control inherent in investing, either. Making a million dollars that way would mean rising and falling with the whims of the market, and I wanted to carve my own path.

At the age of twelve, I concluded the only way to make a million dollars on my own terms was to start a business. My adventure hit a particularly exciting plot twist nearly twenty years later. One *very* surreal morning at the age of twenty-nine, I found myself staring in awe at a bank balance that had multiplied overnight into eight figures.

That morning, my business partner, Matt, had called early. I'd known Matt all through my twenties, and our individual adventures had taken the same path for much of it—we'd built businesses together, stayed up into the wee hours talking about politics and religion, shared our biggest wins and most crushing losses, and even become fathers in the same year. Our relationship, like any business partnership, was a lot like a marriage. We had a rule that no matter what was going on we'd always pick up the phone if the other called.

When I answered the phone, Matt sounded happy. He hadn't sounded happy in weeks—we'd been going through a stressful time with our business, probably the most stress either of us had experienced up until that point. But his voice then sounded like he was barely holding back the biggest grin of all time.

"Did you see it?" he asked.

I knew right then what he was talking about, but I couldn't bring myself to really believe it yet. "It's in there?" I said.

"I don't want to spoil the surprise for you, but yeah. It's in there."

"*Really?*"

"Really."

I opened up my bank's website, logged in, and there it was: $10 million, the most money I'd ever seen in my life. We'd successfully sold a majority stake in our fitness supplement company, Sheer Strength, and the wire from the purchasing company had finally landed. It was ten times more money than my father ever saw over the course of his entire career. In fact, it was enough money that neither Matt nor I would ever have to work a day in our lives again.

"Well, I guess . . . have a good weekend?" Matt said, laughing.

"Oh," I replied, "*I'm gonna.*"

This Has Nothing to Do with Luck

What do you do when $10 million shows up in your bank account overnight?

That's exactly what happened to me and Matt—*but it wasn't by accident*. It was the result of years of direct planning and work. After a decade of trial and error, we achieved the freedom that we'd always hoped to find.

If freedom is your goal, then this book is your starting point. Throughout your journey, this book will be your guide, taking you through every step of building a million-dollar business and helping you overcome each hurdle. I've already experienced these hurdles many, many times, as have other entrepreneurs I've worked with, and so have the students who follow the methods I lay out in my podcast and YouTube videos. We've walked the road ahead of you, so we know where the potholes are.

Actually, that's part of why I wrote this book; it fires me up to know that I can help other entrepreneurs have a smoother journey on their own path to freedom.

Matt and I didn't have a guidebook when we were building our business. We did have a mentor, Travis, an incredible human who helped us a great deal. No one we knew had ever built a million-dollar business, let alone *sold* one. In fact, most of the "entrepreneurs" we hung out with were more like "want-repreneurs." They were the kind of entrepreneur you see on YouTube these days showing off their "wealth" with cars and girls. (Lesson Number One: Nobody has ever gotten rich by spending all their cash on luxury automobiles. Lesson Number Two: Having a girlfriend does not make you rich—it's usually the opposite, in fact.)

That was never our scene. We wanted something real. Matt once said to me, "I *know* we're going to be successful. We'll work hard at it until we do. Whether it's this idea or not, I don't know . . . but we'll get there." If you can build that same mindset, you're going to be just fine.

As longtime "aspiring entrepreneurs," we'd seen plenty of ideas come and go. We saw many want-repreneurs come and go, too—we outlasted them one by one. We tried countless business models and "good ideas" in our attempts to achieve success. And we even had fun doing it. Honestly, the easiest—and possibly the most fun—time of being an entrepreneur is the very beginning, when you're amped up on excitement. You stay up late at night just as Matt and I used to do, talking about all the amazing success you're *going to have*. You dream about the day your bank account is suddenly going to explode tenfold overnight. These blustery, late-night conversations happen between nineteen-year-old business nerds all over the world every day, and they usually lead to jack squat.

With Matt and me, those conversations led to *many* false starts and failed ventures. We laugh about them today. It took us six years to be ready; another year to come up with the idea for the method you'll learn in this book; and four years to build out the model that ultimately led to our $10 million payday.

But if you take the steps that you'll learn in this book and go all in, it won't take ten years to be successful. It'll take you just twelve months.

Matt and I were the first to "pioneer" this method, mostly cobbling it together ourselves through sheer determination and hours upon hours of research and testing. Since we put it into practice and started to teach it to others, it has helped create hundreds of success stories. You'll meet the entrepreneurs behind many in this book. Looking at the $10 million in my bank account that day was the moment I knew for sure Matt and I hadn't just come up with some little side hustle on the internet. This wasn't some passive-income scheme. This was real.

When we sold Sheer Strength to an investment company—and had multiple interested parties in the process—it really clicked for me. I realized, *This method works. It's scalable. It's repeatable. And big businesses want to buy what it creates.*

And if you decide to put yourself through the soul-sucking struggle that is entrepreneurship, you can be successful, too.

Go All In

Take another look at the title of this book.

What does *12 Months to $1 Million* immediately conjure in your mind?

If the answer to that question is *an easy path to getting rich*, or *a quick way to make a few grand on the side*, then this is going to be a tough year for you. You would probably be better off with a lottery ticket instead of a business. Make no mistake: What I'm offering you in this book will require a lot of work. You can't do this casually; while you can start it on the side, it's not a "side hustle" or a onetime gig. At some point you'll need to go *all in*. When you do that, building a million-dollar business becomes possible.

At the foundation of every successful business is one entrepreneur who is willing to put it all on the line and take the company to its first million. When change happens and wealth is created, there's always one person who puts it on his or her back and takes it on as a challenge.

I live to empower that person. Contrary to what you might hear in the media, profit-driven capitalists create the greatest change in this world. I believe in this ethos so strongly that I personally invest in the businesses my students and friends start; I want to be part of the change these entrepreneurs create.

People like Hanny, who discovered my podcast and started an outdoors company I fell in love with. I invested $85,000 in her handmade backpack company, NeatPack. And companies like Onnit, a performance company started by my friend Aubrey Marcus that has become the most-loved human performance company in its industry. Or Outstanding Foods, a mushroom-based chip company that's part of a movement to create delicious snack foods in a sustainable way. Every day I spend my time advising startups and empowering entrepreneurs to build amazing things.

Throughout the long years Matt and I spent building our method, I documented our experiments and all our many iterations, failures, and successes, on my podcast and on my YouTube channel. The more I shared, the more others followed along and started sharing their journeys as well. An entire community of internet entrepreneurs began to form as we compiled hundreds of case studies, personal journeys, and stories of incredible success and crushing failure. Together, we all found our way.

After Matt and I sold our company, I started Capitalism.com, which empowers entrepreneurs to create change through business. I also started an annual event, the Capitalism Conference, where I bring together all the top entrepreneurs from whom I most want to learn and have them tell their stories to entrepreneurs like you.

With the 12 Months to $1 Million method, we've inspired a community of entrepreneurs who are impacting their corners of the world, and I want you to be a part of that community. Hundreds of people have told me that they built seven-figure businesses as a result of listening to the free information that I publish on the internet.

All of this is a way of saying that there are people rooting for you. We want you to succeed. But it's a huge responsibility. You have to commit. You have to go all in.

I get approached by a lot by people looking for advice or to share the story of their business. You'd think this would get old quick, but honestly, *it doesn't*. I love talking about entrepreneurship with people who are just as passionate about it as I am. I especially love talking about the tough stuff, the downfalls and struggles. It's the kind of stuff you just can't possibly understand unless you've been there.

The one thing that drives me crazy, though, is when people approach me for advice on a foolproof, zero-risk, "easy way" to be successful. Regardless of what the internet tells you, *this doesn't exist*.

If you're only pursuing the result, you're going to have a tough journey. If you are only focused on the "someday goal" of having a million-dollar business, then you will overlook the work that is right in front of you and fail to reach your goal at all.

In this book you'll learn why you have to go through each step in order, one by one, to achieve your goal—and why shortcuts will actually crash you into the side of the proverbial mountain. Expect your fair share of bad days, self-doubt, and confusion along the way. We will overcome most of your challenges together, but for the next twelve months expect a lot of long hours with no pay, countered by infrequent moments of deep joy, excitement, and passion.

If you take away one thing from this book, though, it should be the deep realization that *you can do this*. You can come out the other side with a profitable business that sets you free for the rest of your life.

12 Months to $1 Million

I'm going to repeat the following many times throughout this book. In fact, by the time you finish reading, you'll have it memorized—it's that important. Here's how you build a million-dollar business:

If you have three to five products, at an average price point of $30 per unit, each selling twenty-five to thirty units per day, you have a million-dollar business.

When I tell people this simple formula, their eyes widen. They often don't believe me.

"Seriously?" they say. "That doesn't sound so hard. That sounds easy!"

As far as what to sell, this process will theoretically work for any type of business. That being said, I've seen the most success selling physical stuff—or, as I call it, *building a brand*. A brand is simply a group of products (three to five), each of which serves the same customer.

It's not complicated to follow the process I lay out, but it takes work to get there. The process includes a series of steps that can't be skipped. Imagine building a million-dollar business like building a house. You have to carefully follow the blueprint, or the whole thing falls apart. You can't just skip putting in the foundation in favor of painting the walls.

In the chapters that follow, here's what you'll discover:

1. Opportunity. What is the best opportunity for a new entrepreneur to build a successful business? Why is now the time to do it? How does the new landscape of e-commerce and social media create an environment of opportunity? And how do you fit into it all? You will discover why now is the perfect time to create your pie, and why there are others who are ready and willing to buy a slice.

2. Mindset. There's a reason not every wantrepreneur becomes a successful entrepreneur, and psychology is a big piece of the puzzle. I'll take you through the development of the right mindset to take a business from zero to one million in a year.

3. Getting customers. A million-dollar business doesn't start with a product; it starts with a person. Your first step in building your business must be identifying your *customer*, and then answering his or her need. This builds a real brand, not just a revenue stream. If you get this piece right, you will have droves of repeat buyers who will eagerly "overpay" for your products, thank you for it, and tell all of their friends about you.

4. Product. Choosing your first product will be the biggest hurdle you face. It will take research, patience, and determination. Most importantly, it will require *listening to what your customer is saying*. I'll take you through the whole process, from ideation to prototyping and refinement, helping you clear this hurdle in no time flat.

5. Funding. Sure, you've got a great product, and you know to whom you're selling—but how do you fund your inventory? Here's how to bootstrap, borrow, and build your way to a self-sustaining revenue machine, without stressing about money.

6. Stacking the deck. How do you nearly *guarantee* that your first product is successful, right out of the gate? Once you've decided what business you're in, we will work to ensure that you don't get stuck holding a product no one wants; this is where you stack the deck so your launch day is set up to blast off.

7. Launch. Your first product is ready to launch. What do you do now? Do you just let it ride? *No.* Here's where building relationships and a few strategic marketing tips will take your business from a single product to a world-class brand, as we cover what you need to do to reach the key growth point of twenty-five sales per day.

8. Scaling. You've got one product selling twenty-five units a day. You've proven you can get a product up and selling in the marketplace. Now it's time to launch products two, three, four, and five and watch the snowball build into a million-dollar revenue stream by the end of twelve months.

9. Marketing. Sure, if you're friends with a ton of celebrities who will post about your brand on their Instagrams, you're all set with marketing. But what if you're starting from scratch, with no contacts and no marketing experience? Here's how you can build the right kind of marketing through relationships, influencers, and audiences, bringing your business to the level of a respected brand.

10. Acquisition. What does it look like to sell your business? There are many buyers out there hungry for what you're building. Here's where you'll learn how to navigate the process, lock in your payday, and decide what to do afterward.

For many of the entrepreneurs I work with, when it comes to starting a business, it's not their first rodeo. Trouble is, they can see the hundreds of different routes to financial freedom. They often dabble in a few: For a while, they dance with real estate investing; then they try Kindle publishing; then they land on affiliate marketing. It goes on and on. That confusion keeps them stuck. They can clearly see the various business models they can choose from, but the *choice* is the obstacle. There's a lack of clarity around which model (or which product, or which direction) will get them all the way to their destination.

The method outlined above is exactly how to get there. I run an accelerator called The Backroom, which is for entrepreneurs who have crossed the $1 million mark (that will be you by the time we finish). Together, we open up new opportunities, and my ultimate goal is to work with the businesses that excite me most, join as a minority partner in the company (usually 20 to 40 percent), help the business grow from seven figures to eight figures, and get ready to sell the company.

Some of our members have sold for $9 million, $20 million, even $50 million. I have another member who just received a $50 million valuation and another who is building a $100 million portfolio. All of them started exactly where you are right now—finding this plan, absorbing the method, and beginning the process of building their first million-dollar business.

Many of them got there in about a year, and they didn't have this book. You do. One year from now, you may find yourself in my living room, working with me inside my community, and readying your business to be sold for an amount of money that will change your entire family's life.

That's my secret, selfish reason for writing this book: Many of you'll end up being great people I want to work with, building great businesses I want to take part in.

I had my day and got my big win. To get to where I want to go next (more on that later), I'll need to create a lot of success stories in the process. I like to think of what we are building at Capitalism.com as an online *Shark Tank* for entrepreneurs bold enough to create change in their lives and get rich in the process (or, at the very least, financially free).

Before You Begin: What I Wish Someone Had Told Me

With this book in your hands, you have an advantage. You have the benefit of everything it took me ten years, and much failure, to learn. You have the stories of dozens of entrepreneurs just like me who have happily shared their own journeys in the hope that they can save you some stumbles.

Distilling everything I wish I'd known when I started this journey took me a long time, but I believe the following six nuggets of wisdom would have set me up for a *much* faster—and less painful—road to success.

1. This is harder than you think.

Becoming and succeeding as an entrepreneur is a lot like parenting. I can *tell* you that it's hard; you can read books—like this one—that explain all the pitfalls and provide all the tips; but at the end of the day, you just *cannot* imagine how difficult it will be.

Ask any parent and they'll tell you the same thing: Raising children is harder than they ever thought. A lot of people start a family because they think it will bring a new level of love and fulfillment to their lives. They're not wrong. Being a parent has been and will always be a source of limitless joy. That being said, parenting is ten times harder than one ever imagines, and there's no real way to prepare for it. (Life tip: Thank your parents. For those of us lucky enough to live today, we owe so much to our parents, who gave up so much just so that we could have a shot at this. They did the best job they could, and any scars from childhood will only give you more fuel to succeed.)

The people who think that the "entrepreneur life is easy" almost always fail. More accurately, they think it will be easier than they've been told. After all, how hard can it be to hustle for twelve months for a million-dollar payday? You have to nurture your business. You have to live with it every hour of every day. Like a child, sometimes it calls for you in the middle of the night, and you have to get up to help it.

People who plan for an easy ride get kicked in the teeth and quit. Even if you enter knowing how hard this can be, you'll find the reality surprising. But knowing the challenges from the start gives you a much better shot to build something that works.

2. It's not about what you can *get*, but what you can *create*.

One of the first mindset shifts you'll need to understand is the difference between value *extraction* and value *creation*.

Too many people think they are only out to get their slice of the pie, of the "limited" value out there in the world. They walk up to a table that has a single pie, take a slice, and think that's enough. They imagine that once all the slices are gone, that's it. No more value.

That's why people hate on billionaires, or companies that don't pay enough taxes: They believe that the "top 1 percent" get rich by taking from others.

The truth is that we create value. For every slice you take, you have to bake a whole other pie. Jeff Bezos got insanely rich because he changed an industry. That's value creation.

Far too many people come up to me and ask, "How do I get my slice of the pie?" That's the dog-eat-dog world. That's hustling for every dollar. Stop thinking about what you can take, and start recognizing the value you can *create*. Money, which is a by-product of good work, will flow to you as soon as you make that switch.

3. Growth is like interest: It compounds over time.

A hustler lives from small win to small win.

Tiny wins—buying things at garage sales and selling them on eBay— never *compound*. You might work really hard and make extra money, but it's unlikely you'll become a millionaire.

If you follow my plan, results will stack extremely quickly. They might seem insignificant at first, but, after a year, you will have a hard-charging income stream that continues to grow for years to come.

One of my favorite books is called *The Slight Edge* by Jeff Olson. In it, he argues that extraordinary results do not come from big wins—they come from incremental steps forward that compound over time. For instance, you don't get fat by overeating one time; you get fat when you consistently overeat.

The same is true with wealth. You don't get rich with one big sale. You get rich by doing the right thing long enough for it to compound.

In my experience, it takes about twelve months of consistent, compounding efforts to create a successful, profitable business. Everything we do in life, and all the success we have, comes from habits. More to the point, it comes from setting long-term goals and using those habits to drive toward them. Whether I'm trying to get fit, get rich, or get happy, I need to think long term.

If I treat my customers well, they'll be happy. If my customers are happy, they'll leave good reviews. Good reviews build a loyal customer base. Efforts and actions compound, and the more long term you can think, the more successful you will be.

4. Your business impacts more than your bank account.

I wish someone had told me, way back when I was getting started, just how big this was all going to get. I had no idea what I was building or what it would all mean years later. Had I known, I would have gone even harder. I would have been even more aggressive.

You'll soon discover that big brands are out there, looking to acquire small brands to gain market share. They are literally *banking on* entrepreneurs like you to build something great so they can jump on board. I never knew how many people were rooting for me. I never knew this process could inspire so many people, or that I would take those same people on as students and watch them transform their lives based on my designs.

Even beyond that, your business directly impacts *your customers*. We all have brands that we are passionate about—for me, it's Quest Nutrition and Zevia—and we love to buy. You will be building something that directly impacts people on that level.

People get into this life thinking too small. They want the added revenue stream, they want a little extra, and they have no clue just how big this can get. There are a million dominoes ready to fall, and all it takes is someone with the drive to push the first one.

Every micro-decision is a reflection of what happens at scale. I might make nine videos that get a hundred views a piece, but my tenth video is seen by 100,000 people. One out of 100 videos will go viral and be seen by millions.

That's why it's a good idea to treat every customer well every single time. Nine out of ten are going to say, "Thanks for my thing." One is going to brag about you to ten of their friends, though, and one out of 100 is going to have an influencer following of 10,000. One out of 1,000 is going to be a retail partner who's buying you to see if they want to have you in its thousand stores. Every roll of the dice matters.

5. Having a partner can be a blessing or a curse (if done wrong).

You may decide to go into this business with a partner. After all, I had Matt by my side in building, scaling, and selling Sheer Strength, and it felt just as good to share success with him as it did to have his help when things went wrong.

Great partnerships are not 50/50—they are 100/100. You have to punt the expectation that you will each do an equal amount of work because there will be times when you drive the ship, and times when your partner carries the torch.

If you can take total and full ownership for your own results, then I would highly suggest bringing on a partner with the same mentality. When two people come together, and they both take total responsibility for the results of the project, it can be magical.

It can also be a disaster if it's the wrong fit.

It's important to understand the difference between a friend and a partner. Sure, you can form a company with your buddy, have a lot of fun during meetings, and maybe make a few bucks. If you're lucky, the stars will align, and you'll have a functional work relationship that leads to company growth. Most likely, though, you'll end up like the majority of entrepreneurs: broke and starting from square one.

There are two types of entrepreneurs: those who drive the vision and those who build. It is incredibly rare for one person to be both a Visionary and a Builder. Visionaries are highly energetic and highly emotional; they come up with new ideas. In contrast, Builders are stable, organized, and calm. Visionaries make horrible managers, so people usually hate working with them. But they are great at selling and making big, bold decisions. Builders rarely think big, but they are fantastic at managing details and ensuring that nothing falls through the cracks. A Visionary needs a Builder to get anything done, and a Builder needs a Visionary to build something that matters.

When you bring these personalities together, they can accomplish great things.

For example, take another former business partner of mine, Sean. We built and sold a small yoga business a few years ago. While we were in the initial building phase, he couldn't get his head out of the planning process, and he wouldn't make any decisions. He's the Builder; I'm a Visionary. Every time he got stuck, I pushed us toward the next step. It forced him to play catch-up. At the same time, his need to be prepared meant we always had answers to any questions that arose. Together, we built an actual business. We balanced each other out.

To this day, Sean says, "If it wasn't for you, I'd still be looking at spreadsheets, trying to decide what product to sell."

I reply, "Without you, I'd still be thinking a year into the future, about how to scale a million-dollar business I haven't even built yet."

A general rule of thumb: If your partner has the same qualities that you have, then one of you is unnecessary to the business. It's called a partnership for a reason. Both of you need to bring an element to the table. If one of you is the operator, the other needs to be the big thinker. If you're great at networking, the other person needs to understand logistics and operations. You need to have complementary personalities, total trust, and the same goals. Sean is the most humble, balanced, kindest human being ever, and he wouldn't have gotten anywhere without crazy old me. I'm a spacey, emotional, overly optimistic driver, and I wouldn't have gotten anywhere without him.

6. No matter what, the chips stay on the table.

Despite the "going all in" analogy, I don't compare this life to gambling. In this game, the house doesn't win because you stayed to play. Being an entrepreneur means thinking in *years* rather than *months*. The worst thing you could do in any cycle is trade a long-term risk for a short-term win.

When it comes to building a seven-figure business, here's the mindset you should take on: The longer you can keep your chips on the table, the bigger your end result is going to be. This means *not* taking an income from the business as soon as you're profitable. It means keeping the profits in play for the business rather than for your own bank account. Put simply, it means *reinvesting* rather than *recouping.*

The time frame I recommend for reinvesting profits is a year, at least. During that year, you'll be working for very little payoff. You'll be putting every dime you make back into the business. If you can stick it out, then you will increase your chances of success exponentially.

Your Twelve Months Starts Now

I tell my students to prepare for a year because that's how long it takes.

That year isn't spent sitting around. You're working, growing, and building toward your goals. Those habits you develop only grow stronger, and that time builds up quality exponentially. Think about it like compound interest. Let's say you sell your business after six months and make $100,000 on the sale. Just imagine how much more you could have made had you waited and kept building for the entire year. You could have grown into new markets, cemented your customer base, and improved on your product list. By giving in to the appeal of a short-term payout, you've potentially cost yourself millions.

For some of you, the big question is surviving that first year. You have bills to pay and at least yourself to support. Holding off for a long-term payout can be grueling. Later on, we'll discuss methods you can use to fund your endeavor, but those aren't guarantees either. Your first year may be entirely on your shoulders. You might have to work a job you hate while sinking every waking hour into your business.

Author and trainer Craig Ballantyne famously said, "Success is simple once you accept how hard it is."

To set your expectations, I often split the twelve-month process into three stages: The Grind (months one to four), The Growth (months five to nine), and The Gold (months ten to twelve).

Most people fail because they never make it out of The Grind. Those are the initial months in which you make decisions around what product to sell, what your price point will be, and what launch strategy you will use. You're in The Grind until you can sustain at least twenty-five sales per day on your first product.

This book is designed to get you out of The Grind as quickly as humanly possible. If you follow the steps outlined, you will leave The

Grind about four months after you finish reading. Your challenge will be making fast, bold decisions, and being okay with them being less than perfect. Otherwise, you will overthink every step, and you will stay stuck at "Stage Zero," the state in which you're just *thinking about becoming an entrepreneur.*

At the beginning stages, speed is your friend, and every sale, review, and comment matters a great deal. When you have a following of about a thousand people, and you have at least twenty reviews on your first product, you will likely get to twenty-five sales per day quickly.

The second stage is The Growth, which is where the snowball really starts to build. Your job in this stage is to roll out as many products *as you can comfortably handle,* without distracting yourself. Remember, just three to five products at twenty-five sales per day is a million-dollar business.

In this stage, you'll be releasing new products to the same group of customers as your first product. You will release them, one by one, and get each product to at least twenty-five sales per day. Momentum will build faster here as you won't have to go through the same "decision hurdles" the second time around. About six months in, you'll be able to smell seven figures, and you'll be tempted to complicate the process. Fight your urge to get distracted, at least until you've released a minimum of three products.

The third stage is The Gold. Here you'll start to experiment with different advertising formats: You might run some Instagram ads, sponsor a podcast, or pay an influencer. This is also the stage in which you finally, *finally,* might consider paying yourself, and you can call yourself a full-time entrepreneur. However, until you are at this point, your job is to stay as laser focused on *following the plan* as you can.

There will be days when the sacrifice is excruciating. There will be days when you know you'll have a six-figure windfall if you just sell and walk away. Hold on. You *can* survive another few months, another few quarters, until you've reached your goal.

After all, the title of this book isn't *Six Months to $1 Million.*

Prepare yourself for one hell of a year.

1

The Landscape of Opportunity

One of the most common questions I'm asked is "Am I too late? Is there still opportunity, or have I missed the boat?"

Trends change, fads come and go with the wind, and it can sometimes feel like you're always chasing relevancy. While it's true you need to keep up to date to stay in the game, the tempo is a lot more manageable than one might think.

I started my first business on my parents' dial-up computer, handcoding websites in raw HTML and Dreamweaver (if you know what that is, you're officially "old" in internet years). I built websites, got them to rank in Google, made some money, and used it to pay for college. Then Google went through some changes, and I had to adjust. The puck keeps moving. You keep learning. You keep growing.

Some people resist marketplace changes because their primary income stream feels under threat. At the same time, those changes open up new opportunities. Today, there are more available tools and opportunities than ever.

When I started my first businesses, there were no website tools to help you launch a site in just a few minutes. There was no social media. There was no YouTube. There was no way to "get your name out there."

You'd think that when those things came about, everyone would have rejoiced, right? *Finally, an easy, fast, free way to build your audience!* But guess what? For every one person celebrating, there were two complaining. People feared that social media would put the bloggers out of business. They thought that Facebook would kill email marketing.

Change is inevitable. But with those changes always comes new opportunity, so there's no such thing as missing the boat.

For example, Amazon's Fulfilled by Amazon program, or FBA, was one of the greatest developments of the 2000s. FBA made it possible for any person on the planet to quickly and easily open his or her own store, and Amazon would do all the fulfillment from its warehouses. Don't underestimate how massive this shift was: For the first time in history, you could open up a store on the internet's version of Fifth Avenue, pay zero rent, and be in front of millions of customers.

For the first few years on FBA, it was the Wild West. It was easy to rank for keywords, and the competition was low. Hustlers poured onto the scene selling everything from iPhone cases to kayaks. Anything that you put on Amazon.com would sell because FBA made it so wide open. As my mentor Travis put it, it was so wide open that "idiots got rich."

When you have a massive shift like that, you almost always have a Wild West period, followed by a big correction or consolidation. For years, I warned my listeners and followers to use the opportunities on Amazon to build a real brand. Those who did made millions of dollars. Those who did not got swallowed up when bigger players came onto the scene selling spatulas for 50 cents cheaper than they were.

As that landscape changed, people started complaining it wasn't "easy anymore" or that the opportunity on Amazon was gone. Well, *yeah*—like anything, the puck had moved, but new opportunities continued to open.

Here's the truth: If you are building a business online, you have more opportunities than ever before. When Amazon was a Wild West, there was no Kickstarter, which makes it possible for you to fund your business with nearly zero dollars. And there was no Instagram, which makes it possible to put your product in front of tens of thousands of people in a heartbeat. We'll cover all these opportunities in future chapters. For now, just know that there will always be opportunities, and we are still only in the second inning of the internet business landscape.

Furthermore, there is always a demand for good products and good brands. I mean if Folgers—objectively crappy coffee—can continue to be a billion-dollar brand, then there is opportunity for you, too. The landscape will continue to change, and competition will always be a part of the process, but you can still win, *especially* if you put these steps to work.

Why Old Brands Buy New Ones

Kimberly-Clark is a huge, publicly traded company that specializes in paper products. They cover everything from personal hygiene products to family care. You probably know them as the parent company for Kleenex and Cottonelle.

Now, if you were the CEO of Kimberly-Clark, and you wanted to sell your products as they did from 1975 to 2006, then you'd run a bunch of ads on TV. That was where the media lived; that was the best way to reach a wide band of customers. Kimberly-Clark handles all its manufacturing and distribution internally, and no other company can compete with that.

But today, the game has changed. Especially for the big brands.

A student named Norm can build a seven-figure business selling party hats from his dorm room now. He can pay someone overseas to make a product specifically for, say, a Batman party. Then he can directly market to parents holding superhero parties for their three-year-olds. If Norm continues to expand his business, a major paper company might come calling. They will see that Norm has a tiny monopoly on paper Batman hats, and they will want to own that distribution.

In fact, that's the strategy *most* of the big brands follow. They buy other brands to expand their market share.

It used to be that big brands owned everything. It was impossible to compete with any brand because they owned the distribution and the advertising. But the internet—especially Amazon, Shopify, Kickstarter, and Facebook/Instagram—changed all that. Now it's possible for small shops to quickly hit pay dirt. You just need to define your space and build your business for a specific market. The monopoly on distribution is gone.

As a result, one- and two-person businesses can start selling a handful of products on Amazon, Shopify, Kickstarter, or social media, and outsell the big brands—at least to their target customer. That creates opportunity for you to get your name on the board in this game. But it's more than just an opportunity for you to build a business. It's also an opportunity to get *noticed* by the big brands and bought out by them.

Why would a big conglomerate like Kimberly-Clark or Procter & Gamble buy a small brand like yours? Very simply put: because they can't innovate as fast as new companies. They're too big and unwieldy. It's kind of like when Facebook bought Instagram, or Twitter bought Periscope. Facebook bought Instagram for $1 billion when it was just nine months old. Why? Because Instagram grew so quickly, it was easier for Facebook to just buy it.

In this new marketplace, instead of building a product and trying to sell it to a business, you're cornering a market for that business to swallow. Small businesses can innovate a lot faster than major brands. They can product-test via social media engagement. They can make targeted changes to their products according to what their audience is telling them.

Kimberly-Clark can't reconfigure its entire product line because a few Amazon reviews expose a pain point. At this point, they're simply too complex to roll with the changes requested by individual customers. But *you* can.

Just ask Peter Rahal, the founder of RXBAR, a "real food protein bar" made for athletes who want to keep their diets clean. Peter founded RXBAR in 2013 in his parents' basement. The red food mixer that he used to blend together dates, nuts, and eggs is still on display at the company's Chicago headquarters.

It's not as if there was a lack of protein bars on the planet; endurance athletes had their bar—it was called the Clif Bar (and that business, too, followed the "recipe" in this book). Low-carb dieters had Quest bars. Bodybuilders had MET-Rx bars and PowerBars. It seemed like the world didn't need another food bar, or even another packaged snack, but there was no food bar *specifically* for CrossFit athletes, Peter's target customers.

Just three years after founding RXBAR, Peter got a call from Kellogg's. Kellogg's knew that it couldn't make a good company as quickly as Peter had already done, so they bought him out instead. Kellogg's paid young Peter, then just three years into his entrepreneurial journey, $600 million. In financial terms, we call that "a good return on investment."

Chances are you've eaten an RXBAR, or a Clif Bar, or a Quest bar, even if you aren't a CrossFit athlete or a bodybuilder. And that, again, is the difference between brands and products. Products appeal to one person at one time. But a brand appeals to a group of people *first*, and then gets adopted by everyone else. Products make a little bit of money for a short amount of time. Brands get acquired for millions of dollars.

The Online Brand Cycle

I mentioned being in the second inning earlier. Right now, we're still in the early stages of this new cycle of online brand creation. The first wave started with people buying on Amazon; the ease of using that website made it possible for anyone to sell a product. Then it became possible to create your own e-commerce platform on your business's website using tools like Shopify to streamline the buying process for the customer.

It's not the Wild West anymore, but social media's influence, immediacy, and impact has more than outweighed the value of the freedom of those days. Your opportunity is the same. Anyone who says differently isn't seeing the entire landscape of possibility.

Even previously "untouchable" industries like fashion are being disrupted by entrepreneurs like you.

Recently, I needed to buy new pants. Let me be perfectly clear about something: I have no sense of style whatsoever. I'm a dad, and I dress like one. I've always struggled with fashion—my reference point for being "cool" was wearing my favorite hand-me-downs in high school.

To keep my sanity, I buy simple, comfortable clothing that sort of matches. And I resonate with brands that make this easy for me. Two new-ish brands, Mizzen+Main and Public Rec, targeted me with ads—Mizzen+Main with podcast ads and Public Rec with Instagram ads. It cost them pennies to show up in front of me, and I've spent thousands of dollars with both businesses.

Did I discover them by shopping at a retail store? Nope.

Did I discover them through TV ads or even from a friend's recommendation? Nope.

I discovered both with tiny niche advertising that cost those companies next to nothing—and now I buy their clothes and tell all my friends about them. In fact, the founder of Mizzen+Main, Kevin Lavelle, spoke at one of my Capitalism Conference events, where he shared how he built the company. There was no clothing line specifically for active men, and wearing traditional dress attire felt restricting, so he made the company for himself and people like him. And it took off like a rocket.

While new companies like Public Rec and Mizzen+Main were growing in market share, industry leader Diesel—a major clothing brand that reigned supreme for decades—filed for bankruptcy. This is where we are in the cycle: Small brands grow quickly, and big brands are scrambling to keep up. The "old way" of hoping that your product "takes off" is null and void. Today, your idea and your product can partner with the biggest online retailers in the world. To start, you just need to define your audience, launch one product, get it to twenty-five sales per day, and then repeat until you have a million-dollar business.

From there, a new world of opportunities will open up for you.

It was a true sign of the times when Amazon bought Whole Foods in August 2017. This, for the first time, was the merger of the "Old Way" and the new, the first time an internet retailer purchased a physical retailer. Just ten years prior, this would have sounded absurd. Internet businesses don't buy *real* businesses! Internet retailers don't put *real* retailers out of business!

But today your brand may begin by targeting a very small niche—serving a tiny group of people—and expand to the masses very quickly (remember RXBAR) as it's now inevitable that brands that do well online will show up in retail stores everywhere. Think of it this way: If your product wins on Amazon, in a few years it'll be on every shelf of every Whole Foods in the country. Amazon has all the buyer data and will be able to identify if your protein powder is performing well in, say, Atlanta, Georgia. And if it is, they can immediately put it on every shelf at Whole Foods in Atlanta, followed by the rest of the country.

In fact, this is already starting to happen. One of our community members ranked number one on Amazon for a specific weight loss supplement. Soon, it was featured in every Whole Foods across the country. Shortly after, it was picked up by every grocery chain in America. And that's the next stage of this cycle—the merging of the online and offline brands, and the acquisition of the small brands by the big brands.

Moving forward, the key to fast growth is going very, very "micro." The more specific an audience you can target, the faster you will grow. The more "niche" your products, the faster you will be able to release products and get to the first million. If you do that, you will be prepared for the next round of opportunities as they open up. As other major brands start to adjust to e-commerce, more distribution will exist for small brands like yours.

Walmart.com is a great example of an opportunity that will expand in the future. If anyone can compete with Amazon, it's Walmart. It has the infrastructure, the reach, and the recognition. If Walmart is smart, it will take whatever product is killing it on Walmart.com and roll it out in each of its 35,000 stores. That's an audience of millions handpicked to view a proven product. You would do well to pay attention to it.

If you can win on one of these platforms with your marketing, you start to win as a brand. When you prove yourself a viable brand, you get bought up by the big companies. I believe the day will come when Facebook buys a retail conglomerate such as Target; you will advertise on Facebook Marketplace, and the product will be sent from your nearest Target.

The old brands and the new brands are merging, and the world is waiting for your small brand to enter the fold.

How to Create a Billion Dollars with a Tweet

In 2014, the famous investor Carl Icahn wrote on Twitter that he thought Apple stock was undervalued. He said he'd just bought a ton of the underpriced stock.

Apple's stock absolutely soared in the days after that tweet. Carl added billions of dollars to a publicly traded company because he tweeted about it. How does somebody do that? I watched it happen and was absolutely fascinated. He had fewer followers than some news pundits, but he added billions to a company. That's the power of having a responsive audience on the internet.

Investors follow Carl Icahn. When he says a stock is undervalued, his community follows. When you influence the right crowd, you can put any message on the map.

Author and entrepreneur Tim Ferriss is another great example. Tim literally creates trends because his audience is so responsive. There's a famous *Forbes* article titled "The Tim Ferriss Effect," which outlines the growth of brands after Tim mentions them. Many brands can point to record sales days after Tim discusses them on his podcast. In fact, entire brands have been launched on the back of his audience. The mushroom-coffee company Four Sigmatic originally caught fire by advertising on Tim's podcast, and their Amazon sales took off. Today, you'll find them in retail stores all over the world.

The average person on the street likely doesn't know Carl Icahn or Tim Ferriss, but those two guys have enough of a dedicated base to literally put other companies on the map anytime they happen to mention them. Heck, Whole Foods reported running out of stock on a brand of sardines that Tim once mentioned on his podcast.

We live in a world where Kylie Jenner, the youngest sister of the Kardashian clan, can use strategies like this to become the world's youngest self-made billionaire in history. She didn't get there through the reality show she starred on for most of her adolescence. She didn't get there through licensing deals, endorsements, or appearance fees. She got there *exactly* the same way you're going to get there: by using an online audience she built to boost a small internet business into a huge success.

Now I get you're not starting out with the kind of built-in audience Kylie had. For a time, her Instagram was the number-one, most-followed account on the platform. She definitely had a leg up. But in every other way, her process was the same one you're going to learn and use through this book. She identified an audience: young, social media–savvy, beauty-product devotees. She created a brand to serve that audience: Kylie Cosmetics. And she came up with a single launch product that capitalized on her most famous and coveted physical asset: Kylie Lip Kits.

The hype surrounding her product launch was insane. The audience she'd built was so stoked to throw down money for a product that no one had ever even seen that the product completely sold out, earning Kylie $19 million in revenue on the very first day. Eighteen months in, Kylie Cosmetics had earned $420 million in revenue. Within two years, it was valued at $1 billion.

The important takeaway here *isn't* that you need to go start a reality show with your posse of sisters to spend a decade building the kind of online audience that will take you to ten figures in less than two years. The takeaway *is* that, with the right combination of online audience and audience-targeted brand, success is a matter of course.

Start with the Person

You don't have to get a million followers to have a million-dollar business. You need a fraction of advertising and a fraction of brand building along with three to five products that get about thirty customers a day.

At the beginning, that means going "all in" on the few people who notice you, follow you, and buy from you. It will seem trivial at first, but the snowball will build over the next year due to "diffusion."

One of my college professors called it "the diffusion theory of marketing." With every new idea or product, you have a bell curve of adoption. At the very beginning, you have a small but loud group of innovators who talk about a product. Consider your techie friend who buys something new and won't stop talking about it. They talk about it until they get the attention of the early adopters, then the masses, and finally the laggards. Think about smartphones. You had the tech innovators who thought they were cool. They told their friends and brought them in as early adopters. Then, after a few years, even grandma has an iPhone. Now the innovators are moving on to the next thing.

I saw all of this and started to wonder how to use this to my advantage. Could I make enough noise to kick-start the engine toward a million-dollar company?

I'm not Carl Icahn or Tim Ferriss, but I got to thinking about how to use their principles to my advantage. By getting a core fan base for your product, you can write your own check. Take a small group of supporters, or those "innovators" or "early adopters." Combine that with a platform like Amazon, Kickstarter, or Walmart.com. Use social media to sustain a little momentum. Then the snowball really starts rolling toward those hundred sales a day you ultimately want. A few hundred people built into a loyal customer base is all it takes for this business model to be life-changing. That's why Carl and Tim and all these micro-brand examples are relevant.

Identity Marketing and What It Means for You

I have several students who sell coffee. Some work with expensive, high-quality products, so their messaging and market is the hoity-toity, bougie coffee drinker. I have another student focusing on moms, and her entire marketing message is: "Wouldn't the world be a better place if women connected over cups of coffee?"

On the other hand, you have a company like Black Rifle Coffee. If you've never seen Black Rifle's ads, the company is worth a Google (just make sure that there are no kids in the room). Its advertising boldly caters to conservative, gun-owning men who refuse to give their money to "liberal Starbucks." They don't talk about flavors, suppliers, or methods. They simply show themselves shooting guns and invite gun owners to drink their coffee. Their customers eat it up. It's identity marketing, and it works.

What's the difference between Black Rifle Coffee and other coffee companies? When it comes to product, both might be using the *exact same beans*. But the brand, more specifically, *the person they targeted*, is completely different.

If you identify your person and give them exactly what he or she wants, you can build a million-dollar business even if you sell the same type of product that your competitors do. But you won't be competing with them; you will target a *different person*.

A few years back, Miller Lite was losing market share to competitors. Truth be told, it was getting its butt kicked.

The company brought in a professional branding agency to help turn things around and find its new marketing hook. MillerCoors took this agency around its breweries, highlighting everything that went into making its beer. After doing a deep dive on the beer maker's target market and brand story, everyone waited for the new ad.

The marketing company came back with: "Miller Lite: It's Triple Hops Brewed."

Some scoffed at the suggestion, because *all beer is triple hops brewed*.

However, no one else was saying it, so it didn't exist in the public mindset yet. MillerCoors launched the campaign, and sure enough, customers ate up the idea of its "triple hops brewed" beer somehow tasting better than the competition's beer.

Audiences are savvier now, so you have to do more than just market the product. You have to market the customer.

A couple of years ago, I invited Dollar Shave Club founder Michael Dubin to the Capitalism Conference and posted the interview on my podcast at Capitalism.com. Michael told the story of his brand's humble beginnings. Michael hadn't started out as an entrepreneur; in fact, he'd started out as what could probably be termed the polar opposite: a comedian.

Michael honed his comedy for years working with the Upright Citizens Brigade and in various television and film writing rooms. He wasn't looking for a business opportunity at all when, randomly, one fell into his lap. A friend at a party told him he was having trouble moving a huge shipment of razors he'd acquired from Asia. Michael was struck with an idea: What if, instead of trying to get the razors out on store shelves, he cut out the inconvenience of having to go buy this staple item most people he knew used? What if he just shipped them directly to customers' homes?

He knew his exact audience: every guy like him who was fed up with having to pay what seemed like a king's ransom every month for a few cheap blades.

The basics of an idea hatched in his mind. Michael went about setting up the business plan and distribution method. When it came time to launch, he leaned on his comedy background to create a hilarious concept video aimed squarely at the *identity* his company targeted: younger men in their twenties and thirties who wanted a great shave that was both convenient and cheap.

"Are our blades any good?" Michael asks in the first few seconds of the video, having cast himself as the hero of the brand's journey. "No. Our blades are *fucking great.*"

Dollar Shave Club used humor and a brand story to appear to its target audience—to create success right off the bat. It went from selling subscription-service blades to selling a whole suite of inexpensive, convenient, and effective bathroom products, shipped right to the customer's door.

Were Dollar Shave Club razors *that different* from Gillette or any of its competitors? Not at the time. But they targeted a different *person*, and it worked. In 2016, Unilever bought Dollar Shave Club for $1 billion. It wasn't valued on the strength of repackaged razor blades from China. It was valued on Dollar Shave Club's ability to get the attention of its audience and turn it into customers.

Most entrepreneurs fail because they try to make a product for everyone. They waste their money on mass advertising, using messaging that never connects with anyone. If you want people to pay attention, you need to market to a specific *person*, not just *sell your thing*.

If you do this, you might eventually get the attention of a big company that wants to acquire you. A company like Kimberly-Clark may buy one paper company that targets parties, another that targets janitors, and another for families. It's the same with Unilever's purchase of Dollar Shave Club. These big companies aren't just buying up brands—they're buying up *markets*.

In other words, if you carve out a specific group of people and tailor your brand specifically to them, you will attract raving fans *and* the attention of a future acquirer. In this book you're going to learn how to tap into those markets in a way these big companies can't. You're going to make yourself into the most attractive person in the room, and they're going to pursue *you*.

By now, I know you're pumped up and ready to jump into your business. I'm actually a little bit jealous of you. There is no way to go back in time and experience again what you're about to experience. I will be living vicariously through you until I can hear your full story in person.

Before we jump into the step-by-step process, there's a little more context you need to absorb. Having a broad understanding of the opportunity landscape and understanding how identity marketing works for you are important, but they won't get you anywhere unless you first address the space between your ears. Taking the time to evaluate your mindset before going all in is possibly the best investment you could make before starting your entrepreneurial journey.

2

The Mindset of a Seven-Figure Entrepreneur

Most people stay poor for two reasons:

1. They haven't followed a strategy that makes them rich.
2. They don't have the mindset of a wealthy person.

I plan to help you with the first point. I believe the two most important steps to wealth are to build a business and invest the profits. This book will help with the "build a business" part. However, it's up to you to reframe your mindset. The minute you reframe it, own it, and use it as leverage, you have a shot at success.

Remember when I said entrepreneurs are unique? That we see the world differently than other people? I'll go even further with that assessment: Most entrepreneurs have chips on their shoulders. We are eager to prove others wrong. That is why we willingly take on so much stress and risk, betting our money and livelihoods on educated guesses. You might be excited by that idea because becoming an entrepreneur is particularly trendy right now—it's cool to chase your dreams and find wealth and freedom on the other side. A lot of people get into this line of work because they think it means an easy path to millions.

Becoming an entrepreneur often really means twelve-hour days, a lot of red in your bank account, and long nights working alone. It means weathering storm after storm without an end in sight and no one on Earth backing you up.

And no one—I repeat, *no one*—will understand (except, of course, other entrepreneurs). Entrepreneurs tend to be very lonely people, and lonely people often make very good entrepreneurs. We share a particular psychology, and that psychology is *weird*.

Over the years of being an entrepreneur myself, and working with hundreds of entrepreneurs, I've noticed some downright identical patterns in mindset and behavior that can literally predict success or failure. In sharing our personal stories, I've also noticed that a huge number of us share specific life experiences and have carried the incumbent baggage of those experiences into adulthood.

I'd never claim that *every* entrepreneur thinks and acts the same, but there are distinct patterns that play a significant role in how we operate. This isn't a bad thing. In fact, it's usually the secret sauce that leads us to higher levels of financial and creative success than the majority of the population.

Without an awareness of what you're working with, and therefore the ability to guide and harness your mindset to propel you forward, you run the risk that your psyche will hold you back. Any person who truly wants to make a go at a successful million-dollar business needs to do this work on themselves *first,* before they step into building a brand.

Looking Back to Move Forward

When I was eleven years old, my parents separated. I know a lot of kids go through stuff like that, but I took it especially hard. I was a late bloomer, and I already felt out of place at my new middle school. I changed schools, wore oversized hand-me-downs every day, and found solace in computers, where I learned to type 100 words a minute and build websites.

My mom went back to work. My dad left the house and went off to rebuild his life. And me? I would come home from school to an empty house. There I was, my body changing, my world fractured, and I felt alone. That's a lot to figure out with no leadership and no strong role models. (By the way, shout-out to my mom, and all single parents: I never realized as a kid how much her world was shattered at the time. She had been a mom her whole adult life, and now she had to figure out her own life, make money, and give up her dreams. She worked so hard to take care of us. I could not appreciate how hard it was for her until now.)

Searching for male leadership and direction, I clung to male friends and sought out mentors. There were a few men at church who supported and encouraged me, and I dove deep into my church youth group. During that time, I had a friend I really relied on. At a time when I truly needed to belong, he introduced me to the "cool kids" and made me feel like I fit in. I ate lunch with them every day. He helped me make new friends and even got me into some after-school activities. I admired him and followed him around for a year and a half. I dressed like him. I modeled him. I watched TV shows and read books based on his recommendations. I told jokes that I knew would make him laugh.

He was kind, welcoming, and unassuming, and I was so thankful for him. During a time in my life when I felt like I'd been abandoned, he was a steady support. Until one day, when he looked up at me and said, "I find you really annoying. I'm only friends with you because I feel sorry for you."

What?!

He also told me that my other "friends" talked about me behind my back, and that I was never really part of their group.

I remember everything about the moment. I remember the look in his eye and the careless and awkward laugh he let out after he told me all this. I even remember the black long-sleeved shirt I was wearing. I cried when I went home that day, and I can't recall a time that I have ever felt more alone, or more like a loser.

I never went back to the lunch table with those kids. I skipped lunch and hid in the computer lab every day for the rest of the year. For the next four years, I avoided my former "friend" as though he'd physically injured me. I was afraid to even make eye contact with him. During our senior year, I got second place for "Most Likely to Succeed." I lost to him. I hated that he beat me.

Toward the end of that year, he and I were in a small, after-school group together. After four years of carrying around hurt, insecurity, and fear, I worked up the courage to confront him.

We were alone in a classroom, and it was awkwardly quiet. I cleared my throat and said, "Hey, can we talk about that day in eighth grade when we stopped being friends?"

He looked at me funny. "Huh?"

"You know. The day you said you didn't really like me and just felt sorry for me."

"I never said that," he said.

I felt like I'd been slapped. I remembered it so vividly.

"Yes, you did. I've thought about it every day since then."

He said again, "No, I don't remember that. Sorry."

It took everything I had not to scream at him, punch him, or both. "What do you *mean*, you don't remember? I literally hid in the computer lab *every day* after that!"

He shrugged.

I was completely shocked and a little speechless, but I managed one more question: "We haven't talked in *four years*. We were *friends*, dude. Haven't you wondered *why* I disappeared from your life?"

He shrugged again. "I . . . I don't know. I hadn't thought about it. I'm sorry."

And that was that. He claimed no recollection of the incident. To be fair, we were just kids when he said that to me, and when I confronted him, he was eighteen and his life was pretty well set in order. He was a school award winner and headed to a prestigious university in the fall. He had moved on, but I played that conversation over and over in my head for years.

There are two reasons I wanted to tell you this story.

First, every time I share it with another entrepreneur, they nod in recognition. Most entrepreneurs have felt alone at some point in their lives—they all have their own version of my story. A huge number of them are children of divorce, too. A common thread of abandonment, marginalization, and feeling dismissed and devalued seems to run through our experiences. If you're seeing some shade of yourself in my story, I want you to understand you're not alone.

The second reason is actually far more important. If it weren't for that kid, I wouldn't be a millionaire today.

You see, I hid in the computer lab every day because of him. And in that computer lab, I learned to build websites. I learned how to drive traffic. I learned how to write. If it weren't for him, you wouldn't be reading this book. If it weren't for him, you wouldn't go on to build the business that's going to set you free.

My point isn't to preach some platitude about how everything happens for a reason. My point is that there are things in your life that have happened that weren't fair, and while you can't change that they happened, you can turn them into the fuel that will drive you to succeed. Those painful moments are the ones in which you either flee or take a stand and decide to make a change.

Taking Ownership

Maybe it's coincidence. Maybe it's a pattern. Maybe it's universal. But *every* entrepreneur I've met relates to this story, or relates at least to the idea of feeling alone. Suddenly, with no warning or expectation, they had to make all the decisions and live with the consequences. At some point in their lives, they said to themselves: *No one is going to take care of me, so I will take care of myself.* That kind of pressure is a baptism of sorts, and I believe this is where the entrepreneur mindset begins.

An entrepreneur is someone who takes responsibility for a problem and does something about it. Sometimes, that "problem" is that you are broke and don't want to be broke anymore. Sometimes, that problem is that your life sucks and you're finally ready to do something about it. Or your kids have no future, and it's time that you stepped up to the plate, stopped blaming other people or forces, and changed things for the better.

An entrepreneur solves problems that someone else created. An entrepreneur *takes responsibility* in order to *create change*.

I consider every challenge, every painful moment, and everything that I have had to overcome to be a necessary part of the journey. It's an empowering thing when you realize that no one is coming to save you. No one is going to put your life together for you. No one else is going to make you a million dollars.

Some people are held back by a belief that money is scarce and hard to come by. These people allow that belief to form their worldview, which in turn triggers their actions. If you believe money is scarce and hard to come by, you sure as hell won't take the risk of quitting a crappy job to go after a more lucrative but less certain future. You'll take the safe route.

Other people are held back by the belief that making money is self-ish, and that rich people are bad. These people could never become entre-preneurs because the very objective driving a business forward—profit, baby!—is something they can't stomach. They've likely been made to feel bad about it at some point in their lives. They might even project that onto other people and try to make *them* feel bad about making money.

I could give my plan to one person who uses it to build a multi-million-dollar business. I could give the *same* plan to a different person and have them call me a scam artist. Your world is what you believe it is if you choose to take ownership for your worldview and your results.

Quick note: When I talk about "doing the work on yourself," I don't mean just reading this chapter. This is my call to awareness, nothing more. Sit with this, think about it, and take the time to honestly evaluate your mindset.

If that honest self-evaluation brings up any self-doubt or the fear of failure, there is a podcast episode I want you to listen to. It's not about business; it's about slaying these demons. It's called "You Are Enough," and you will find it at Capitalism.com/best.

Take Care of Yourself First

One of my rules of entrepreneurship is to take care of yourself first. I learned this one the hard way by repeatedly working myself into the ground. You are the driver of your business, and businesses reflect their leaders. Your habits, your culture, and your morals all permeate the business and products you create. You must take care of yourself physically and mentally so that you can create and serve others. The most profitable thing you can do is look after the driver: yourself. Entrepreneurship can create stress, and stress breeds bad decisions. You can't force good ideas. That's why my friend Peter Shallard, the self-titled "Shrink for Entrepreneurs," says the primary goal of an entrepreneur is to stay in the mode where work is easy. Eat healthy, get exercise, and take the breaks you need. Taking care of yourself also means taking care of other stakeholders—your customers, your employees, and your investors—and being mindful of your ads and how you interact on social media.

The ends don't necessarily justify the means, either; if you're unhappy with the process, you are likely to be unhappy with the results. When I've worked on ideas in the past, and they haven't been enjoyable throughout, I've never liked the end product. While you should definitely prepare for hard work, you shouldn't have to suffer through misery for an idea.

Here's the difference: If you are working to prove something or to overcome your mental blocks, then you will run into stress, burnout, frustration, and failure. I call it *scaling unhappiness.* However, if you are creating from a place of abundance and genuinely serving others in the process, then life and business is deliriously enjoyable.

When I've been my most successful, I can trace it back to how much I enjoyed the journey. When Matt and I worked on Sheer Strength, we were driven by our passion for the products and the idea of making something we both wanted to buy. Every time we stopped ourselves and listened to the market or new trends, we hit a roadblock. Those bad decisions cost us time and money.

Right now, I'm working on a new food company. The project is a blast, and it's either going to be the most successful thing I've ever done, or the best time I'll ever have on a failure. Either way, the project is enjoyable, and that's a worthy goal. Make sure you're enjoying the ride you're on, or I can guarantee you'll burn out.

The Pursuit Is Worth It

Elon Musk is lonely. He has been public about this. When you're running three companies that are changing the world, you don't have much time for a girlfriend, a social life, or for pretty much anything else. To be perfectly frank, I don't know a lot of balanced entrepreneurs. The happy person with the perfect work–life balance doesn't usually become a rock star entrepreneur.

This game requires you to carry the load on your shoulders and press on in the face of fear. Whether it's your first business or your hundredth, you're going to ask yourself the same questions at some point: *Is this going to fall apart? Am I going to be found out as a fraud? Did one of my competitors already come up with a better version of this?* That little voice breaks most people. True-born entrepreneurs move through it because they've been working through fear their whole lives.

I'm not going to claim that I've never wondered if this is all worth it. In fact, I've spent countless nights wondering if I would be happier if I just had smaller goals. I have family members who encourage me to take extended time off, and every time I do, I feel like the free agent who can't wait to get back into the game.

However, there was one time following the sale of Sheer Strength when I felt particularly depressed about the game of entrepreneurship. I'd made that $10 million payday, but I didn't feel any *happier*. Around that time, I just happened to find myself at dinner with entrepreneur and author Tim Ferriss. He had recently moved to Austin, Texas, and a friend of mine invited me to dinner with him and Tim.

We talked about everything from religion, to business, to relationships, but I had one burning question that I wanted to ask: "Tim, there's one thing that I have to know. You're at the level of success I want to reach. Do you still have days where you wonder if it's all worth it?"

He laughed out loud. "Dude, my family hears me talk about this all the time!"

Then his face changed. He immediately switched to Serious-Tim mode. If you've ever watched his videos, you'll know that he has a very distinct "Serious Tim Face." This was that face.

He looked at me dead in the eye and said, "Ryan, here's what I've discovered. There are plenty of things not worth pursuing. But that doesn't mean that it isn't worth doing. You see, even if the *thing* isn't worth it, *the pursuit is.*"

That sums up entrepreneurship for me.

It's not about the money. It is who you become through the pursuit that ultimately makes this all worth it.

You can start this journey on the side, but as soon as you see "liftoff"—meaning your business is consistently getting sales—that's the time to buckle up and go all in. And it will happen faster than you realize; it's usually four to six months from the start of the business. That's when you are going to dive in headfirst and passionately work twelve-hour days. That will be the norm, but it will be exciting as hell. If you're working a full-time job, that means that your nights and weekends will be full for the next year.

Your pursuit starts with the decision to go all in. It starts with the decision to accept that it is a long journey, and decide to do it anyway. You've likely heard the phrase "freedom isn't free." We use that phrase to honor the fallen heroes who fought for American freedom, as we should. However, we seem to forget that our own freedom isn't free. We have to work *really* hard for it.

As an entrepreneur, you've chosen this life because you want freedom. And if you want a unique life, you will have to sacrifice for it. This journey is going to create challenges. You'll learn new things about yourself—more than you ever thought there was to learn! You're about to open Pandora's Box. In fact, if you think you know yourself right now, check back in six months down the road and marvel at the layers in your soul that you've uncovered.

Let's Roll

Okay. Here we go.

I've given you the context you need to understand what you're getting into, how to become successful at it, and how your life will change.

I've shown you what the opportunity looks like and just how many chances you'll have to make a huge impact. I've shown you why what you're about to build is *massively* in demand, and why people out there are relying on you to build a million-dollar brand.

Hopefully I've raised your awareness and made you think hard about the beliefs and mindset you're bringing to the table and the work you need to do on yourself first to ensure this journey won't see you crash and burn.

There's nothing left to do but show you the method.

In the next several chapters, you'll learn the exact steps—in the exact order—that you need to follow to build a seven-figure business in one year. In each chapter, you'll see how the step looks in practice through real-world stories from myself, my students, and big brands you'll recognize.

Do not skip steps. *Do not* rush to get started before you finish reading. Read carefully and thoroughly, and, if you have questions, seek out the Capitalism.com community online. There's a whole legion of entrepreneurs just like you out there waiting to share their experiences and answer your questions. The relationships that you build during this process will likely become some of the most important relationships of your entire life, so reach out early and start bringing together your tribe.

Most of all, enjoy the journey! Yup, I'm done trying to scare you away—this is going to be *fun*.

3

Step One:
Choose Your Customer

A "million-dollar business" feels impossible to many. It's too big, too bold, and too out of reach. However, I've seen it happen *hundreds of times*, so I know it's completely possible for any entrepreneur with enough drive and commitment. Since most people don't have that, I am often accused of overselling the simplicity of it.

That's why I refer to the first few months of your business as "The Grind." Until you have a product up and selling consistently, every single decision can feel like a mountain you have to climb. This is especially true at the beginning.

If you have no idea what you are going to sell, or you are flat broke, it would be easy to ignore the idea that a seven-figure business is even possible for you.

That was certainly the case with my friend Suzy Batiz.

Suzy had been trying to become an entrepreneur her entire life. She'd started and ended multiple businesses in her youth, and then she went bankrupt—twice.

Her first bankruptcy—at age twenty—was the result of a failed bridal salon. She went bankrupt a second time at thirty, having tried and failed to launch a website that matched recruiters to job applicants based on corporate culture. Like all born entrepreneurs, though, she kept trying. But the next idea wouldn't hit her until she was in her mid-forties. It happened *right under her nose* when her husband stunk up the bathroom. Sometimes, your own biggest problems are signs for very profitable solutions.

It seemed too odd to work: What if there was a way to get rid of the lingering smell in a bathroom after going number two? She started experimenting with fragrance oils, and she soon discovered that odors could be eliminated when her "magic potion" was put in the toilet *before* you pooped.

After a few improvements, she put her magic potion into a spray bottle, and the idea for "Poo-Pourri, Before • You • Go" spray was born.

It was a good idea, and the product worked. But she had one problem: How do you market a product that no one has heard of before? Who's the target customer? After all, as every parent of a toddler who has read that certain kid's book over and over again knows, *everyone poops.*

Suzy got some quick sales by giving the product away to friends and asking for reviews. She gained some traction by word of mouth, and she had a small distribution network in boutique shops. Sales were initially extremely slow, and she feared yet another failure.

However, that all changed when she identified her audience. Suzy's target market wasn't men who stunk up the bathroom (although I'm sure she wished it were!)—it was women like her, who were tired of embarrassing situations.

That was the moment that Poo-Pourri took off.

She filmed a video for the product that featured a prim, English-accented young woman grinning into the camera like a sweet young Mary Poppins while sitting on a toilet, delivering the classic opening line: "You would not believe the motherload I just dropped!"

The video was funny. It was timely. It predominately featured the product. And it absolutely exploded. Within days, Poo-Pourri had launched into the public consciousness, and it quickly became a sensation. Within a few years, Poo-Pourri had done more than $400 million in sales. That was enough to "undo" all the fears of failure that had been brought on by multiple bankruptcies.

Suzy's success is one of the reasons why I brought her in to speak at the Capitalism Conference. Something special happens when you meet someone like Suzy and discover she's just like you—suddenly, things you thought were "impossible" no longer seem so far away.

Suzy is a great example of an overnight success story that took twenty years. Today, she appears on *Forbes's* lists and is a sought-after keynote speaker. What I most admire about her is her ability to inspire entrepreneurs to use their entrepreneurial power to do something *that really matters.*

While Suzy started with a product idea, her business crawled until she identified the *person* who would want to buy it. Once she centered her brand on the person, not the product, her business was off to the races.

That's why, when someone asks me, "What product should I sell?" or "How do I sell more product?" I always answer, "Decide *who your customer is* first."

Focusing on People, Not Products

Back when I started out as an entrepreneur in 2006, no one taught me how to target a person. I discovered it the hard way, and it took me ten years of "failed" entrepreneurship and over-work to finally understand that you can't *really* be happy unless you're doing something that benefits other people. To put it in business terms, you can't be successful until your work is valued by someone else, which is why starting with the person is so important.

I learned to hand-code websites in middle school, using the shared computer in our family living room—on dial-up, no less. Being so plugged into the internet from an early age meant I knew how to do other useful internet things, like basic search engine marketing, internet advertising, and plugging into internet communities, before social media was a thing.

In college, I discovered that I could create pages for products, get them to rank on Google, then run Google AdWords to drive traffic to the site. This was before Facebook, before Kickstarter, and before Amazon turned into the behemoth it is today. Even without any of those tools at my disposal, I did pretty well running this "hustle" from my dorm room. Other kids at school knew I had a successful internet business, and they thought I was hot shit—and, honestly, I thought I was hot shit, too.

That all ended the moment I graduated. I had a way to make money but no clear life path. As a result, my internet business—something I had considered a side hustle, not a career—suddenly felt empty. Sure, I was making enough money to live on, and even invest, but there was no direction to it. There was nowhere else to take the business, and no way to grow it.

On the one hand, I had solved the problem so many of my classmates were facing: *How do I find a job? How do I make a living?* I had money. But I had no purpose, and I had no true skills to scale.

It seems like an overreaction looking back on it now, but at the time, I felt like the world's biggest failure. All that time and money spent on college, and I was . . . what? A guy who sold random products online? An internet traffic manipulator with absolutely no idea what the hell I wanted to do with my life? Yes, I recognize that I had a serious case of "first-world problems," but I felt horribly lost.

One day, I got an email about a meetup in Austin, Texas, for hustlers like me. It was a three-day event about internet traffic and advertising. I had nothing better to do, I had never been to Texas, and I was looking for direction in my life, so I decided to attend.

While I was there, I met other entrepreneurs who were selling *way more* than me. But they were doing something different—they had real *businesses,* not just side hustles.

On one of the breaks, I approached the leader of the summit and asked him for advice. "What would you do if you were me?"

"You know what I would do?" he said. "I would sell *real stuff.* Real products."

It was a huge "aha" moment for me. And the thought of going back to my apartment and staring at a computer screen all day, alone, sounded empty. I decided that I absolutely *must* be around people who were thinking bigger than me.

With no relationship or responsibilities keeping me in one place, I sold almost everything I had, packed the few possessions I had left into the Kia Sportage I'd proudly purchased brand new a few years prior, and drove to Austin, Texas.

I rented an apartment, sight unseen, on a month-to-month basis, and six weeks into my life in Austin, I signed a year lease. I was there to stay. I met a sweet girl at the grocery store. I tried my hand at a bunch of different businesses, thinking that eventually I'd find something I wanted to stick with.

A year into my new life in Austin, the greatest forcing function known to man dropped into my lap: I found out I was going to be a dad. It's incredible how fast a plus sign on a pregnancy test can spin you from lost and depressed to "I have to figure my life out—*now.*"

Until this point, I had been bouncing around, trying my hand at any business opportunity that came my way in a search for purpose and deeper meaning. But that day the plus sign on a pregnancy test announced I'd soon have a daughter named Esther, I decided to put all of my effort into one business model: this one. In a way, I was lucky; my hand was forced. I didn't have the choice *not* to go all in.

Many of you reading this book are probably stuck at the point right before you get into the game, where you have to pick what you're going to sell. Perhaps, like me, you've dabbled in a dozen different business models, and nothing has stuck.

There's a common startup model called "scratch your own itch," and it involves finding a problem you yourself have, solving that problem, and then allowing that solution to form a business. That's what inspired Suzy to start Poo-Pourri.

For years, I did the opposite of this; I sold whatever I could to make money. I did that because it was what everyone on the internet said to do to get rich. They weren't wrong. I made money. And I picked up some useful skills over those years. But there's a difference between making money and building a real business.

You can sell things and make money, and your business will be purely transactional. You can follow a formula that produces profits, and it can work for a while. But once you start thinking about *people*, you start building a real business. If you create something that people actually want, and you communicate to the *person*, you can create a million-dollar business in one year. That's how you become a real entrepreneur.

You're Going to Eat It for a Year

As you build to a million-dollar business in the next year, it'll help you to know the following up front: You're going to eat it for that entire year.

In the first year, you're going to be working for very little money, not drawing a salary, and reinvesting every dollar, until you have a million-dollar business at year's end. By then you'll have a proven concept. Until then, you're figuring it out. Fortunately, I'm giving you the path to help figure it out within the year time frame; without a deadline in place, it's easy to get trapped in passive, *it'll happen when it happens*-style thinking, and that won't serve you.

This chapter is about the foundational decisions *you* need to make to go all in. What is your business? Who is your customer? Knowing the answers to these questions will get you where you want to go faster, so you have to eat fewer shit sandwiches.

This chapter is not just about going all in without a plan. It's about the thought process you'll need to go through to come up with the business you want to go all in on.

You have two ways you can go with this: You can make decisions based on what will bring in short-term cash flow. Or, you can ask yourself, "What is going to bring me the right *customers*, which will lead to a profitable and acquisition-attractive business?"

There's a difference between looking to sell a product and acquiring a customer. Famed business author Peter Drucker said the two functions of business are to *get customers* and to *keep customers*. When you take a sale online, is that getting customers, or keeping them? Most people would say it's the former, but it's a trick question—it's neither.

If they buy on Amazon.com, then they are *Amazon's customer*. If they buy at Walmart, they are *Walmart's customer*. They're not *your* customer until they know who you are, and they choose to come back to *you*.

Who Do You Serve?

I get dozens of messages a day from entrepreneurs, and the most common question I get from people new to the startup process is "What product should I sell?"

To figure out the answer to this question, you first need to understand you're building a brand, not selling products.

Ask someone to define the word *brand*. They're likely to throw out a lot of descriptions: a cool name, a distinctive logo, a website, a great customer service touch they received. Those are all characteristics of a brand, but they're not the foundation of what a brand is. A brand isn't a logo. It's not a fancy website or a pack of sponsorships.

A brand is trust. A brand is an expectation that the customer will be happy with his or her purchase. A brand is something built by creating a group of products that all serve the same person.

My buddy Matt and I both went through serious personal transitions in our late twenties, and we did so at around the same time. As such, we had a shared mindset: We were starting to look toward more adult goals, such as health and longevity. A big component of both our lives was a focus on our health—me, even more so, because by then I had a daughter for whom I wanted to stay healthy.

When it came time to build a brand, we didn't spend a long time wondering what kind of person we should serve with a line of products. We simply looked at our own lives and asked ourselves what we wanted. The answer was incredibly specific: We both wanted a pre-workout supplement that was both effective and free of all the crap that was in every other pre-workout supplement on the market.

It's important to note that we didn't set out with the intention to start a business we were passionate about. Neither of us was passionate about pre-workout energy mixes in any way. All we were doing was developing a product that solved a pain point for us. We were scratching our own itch.

While you don't _have_ to build a brand to serve yourself, it's a good way to start. Knowing your own problems makes it easy to brainstorm solutions. If scratching your own itch doesn't turn you on, think about the people you hang out with—your friends, your family, people at work. Once you think of enough distinct groups, a defined customer will start to reveal him- or herself.

For example, I know a lot of people who tried to make money selling spatulas on Amazon. A few of them did well, but most of them got crushed. Why? Because there are only so many ways to sell more spatulas.

But if you know a lot of moms, and you want to honor the fact that busy moms still want to take an hour to cook for their children, then you can create a series of products for _that person._ One of the products might be spatulas. You start there. Then you can make a line of products that serve those moms. Suddenly, by starting with people instead of products, you have a brand!

People are what make you money, not products. Think of it this way. A product is a onetime transaction. But a brand says something about a person. It tells a story that goes beyond the product. That kind of power leads people to buy multiple products _and tell their friends about them._ If you're just selling random products, you're robbing people of that story— a story about themselves. You're getting _sales_ rather than getting _customers._ And sooner or later, your business will come under threat by the next person who can sell your product cheaper, faster, or slightly better.

In the case of RXBAR, founders Peter Rahal and Jared Smith didn't start out with a burning desire to get into the already flooded protein bar market. They did CrossFit, were friends at the gym, and were dissatisfied with the protein bar options available to them. So, with an incredibly focused customer in mind—their friends at CrossFit—they created a protein bar with "absolutely no BS" aimed directly at CrossFitters.

Starting from a basement headquarters making the bars themselves, they built the brand around their customer avatar, put the ingredients on the front of the packaging, rather than in small print on the back, and watched their product explode. Four years later, they were acquired by Kellogg for $600 million.

It's important to define your customer around someone you know well. Don't pick a group of people you know nothing about unless you're prepared to do a lot of research on them—make sure you can identify at least one pain point shared by the group, and how you can serve that pain point with a collection of products. So, just because you've heard that Gen Z high school students have disposable income does *not* mean that you should target them as your customer. More than likely, you have no idea what that group wants or needs. Who are the people in your life? You know what they want and need.

Once you've identified your person and their pain point or way to help them, it becomes much easier to identify three to five products that can kick off your new business.

A word of warning: The absolute *worst* thing you can do is ask yourself, *What products are super popular right now?* For example, I can't tell you how many people I know chased fidget spinners or tried to sell diet supplements. Both trends exploded brightly, and, sure, some people made some money—but they couldn't build a *business*, because fidget spinners are a one-off product that don't serve a direct person, and diet fads change every year. Those people thought they had a business, but what they actually had was a short-term cash flow machine, and most of those sellers are out of business now that their flash-in-the-pan fad has fizzled out.

If you only think about products based on what's hot right now, you'll eventually be threatened by a mass of competitors, and that's when profit margins get squeezed. Amazon can be the best place to get started selling products, but if you just look at what's selling on Amazon and try to sell that, you'll struggle to build a real business. Why? Well, if someone else sells the same product for $30, you have to sell yours for $28. Then the next person will price his or her product at $26. Now there's a race to the bottom on profit margin.

When you start with people and create products *for them*, you become a price setter, not a price follower. That gives you better profit margins. And you get repeat customers, rather than one-off sales.

How to Choose a Winning Product

If you have a person in mind, it's easy to discover what products he or she will buy.

It used to be that to sell products, you had to develop them from scratch and do a lot of guessing. Companies had to spend thousands on research and development, and then spend millions marketing them via television, newspaper, magazine, and radio ads. After all that, they would then hope and pray the customer would buy the products. There wasn't much else companies could do to affect results or drive growth.

But today, you don't have to guess. You can know if a product will be successful from the very beginning. Sales channels like Amazon aren't just a way to get eyes on your product; they're also a research gold mine.

Right at your fingertips, you have access to all the data you need about how much a product is selling and what customers are saying about it. Just search for the products your person buys, look at what other companies are offering, and pay attention to the reviews. This helps you zero in on exactly who your target market is and what their needs are. What don't they like about this face cream? What's wrong with that instant pot? What are their pain points? How can you improve upon what's already being offered?

Check out Kickstarter and look at projects that raised a million dollars. Go to Amazon and find the best-selling toilet paper. Watch Facebook ads and see what companies are being talked about. You can do this kind of research on any channel where you're thinking about selling, or simply by paying attention.

Your job is to identify three to five products that your ideal person might buy. You don't need to worry about how to make it or how you will sell it—we'll fix that later. Just brainstorm what your person *already buys* and potential things he or she might like to buy. People who do yoga buy mats, towels, and blocks. That's three products. What else might they buy? Clothes, travel cases, or yoga pillows? Do people who do yoga buy other things, too? Like tea, meditation cushions, or essential oil? And do people who do yoga have different shopping habits than others? Do they buy organic, or avoid synthetic skin creams? Write it all down.

You don't need to worry about *how* you're going to do anything just yet—just know that the internet has opened up opportunities for anyone who wants to create something from scratch. Anybody can do a Kickstarter campaign. Anybody can sell on Amazon. Any website can rank in Google. Anyone can run an ad on Facebook. Anyone can post on Instagram and connect with any influencer. Your job is to find out where your customers are, and drop your bait into that pond.

Identify Your Gateway Product

Once you've thought of a target person and are brainstorming at least three to five products that make up your brand, your next step is to start narrowing down the first product you'll sell. I call this the "gateway product" because it's the first in a series of products you'll eventually sell. I like to ask the question, "What product will make my target customer want to buy *more* from me in the future?"

The first product that a yogi buys is a yoga mat. Then he or she buys everything else. So the first product I sold under my yoga business was a yoga mat. One of the first products that a new gym rat buys is a preworkout product. Then he or she buys everything else.

Whether it's yoga mats or sports nutrition supplements, your gateway product represents the first obvious transaction for customers in that space. It addresses an obvious pain point and solves a simple problem. Once the ideal customer has the first product, they are likely to buy other products from the same brand.

Even if your gateway product is the same as everyone else's, you're going to communicate in a way that's specific for your target market. Remember, you're not just selling a product. You're creating a *message*. You're taking something that's already there and crafting a story that's tailored to your customer.

Two people can buy the same product for completely different reasons. Somebody who's buying gloves to work in the garden might buy the exact same gloves for woodworking or going to the gym. Their preference would be to find a brand that speaks directly to them. Put simply, customers want to buy into brands that are going to serve them over the long term. You're not just selling workout gloves. You're selling to *people who work out*. This is nonnegotiable.

Dave Asprey from Bulletproof Coffee is my favorite example of someone who did this extremely well.

Dave started as a humble blogger who wrote about productivity and health optimization. He built a reputation by defending the health benefits of coffee and encouraging readers to add fats and oils to their morning brew.

A few years into his journey, he launched his own coffee—Bulletproof Coffee. That was his gateway product. Is his coffee special, compared to other coffees? Some say so, because it's made *just for them*. It's organic, certified mold-free, and twice the price.

If Dave had simply wanted to start another coffee company, his second product would have been something like a dark roast or a new flavor. But Dave had his attention on something bigger, and he had three to five products outlined from the start.

The second product he launched was a coconut-based MCT oil to go into your special brew mold-free coffee. Then he launched lactose-free, grass-fed ghee, also to add to your coffee, to "slow the absorption of caffeine, which gives you even energy for several hours." Then it was protein bars, then whey protein, then *upgraded* MCT oil. Now Bulletproof is a bio-hacking company worth hundreds of millions of dollars.

Dave had three to five products in mind from the get-go, all of them designed to serve his target market. That's very different than just selling coffee.

Like energy bars, the coffee market is incredibly saturated; but it becomes *far* less saturated when you serve one of your target market's pain points. "Upgraded coffee," reads Dave Asprey's blog, "[uses] a proprietary Bulletproof Process™ to create coffee that is tested to be *lower in mold toxins that inhibit human performance*."

Bulletproof focused on the pain preventing its customers from being high performers. As a result, everyone from CEOs to professional athletes to busy parents started buying from Bulletproof. What did these different groups have in common? Simple: They wanted higher performance. They were all Dave's target customer.

People buy products that say something about themselves. Paying twice the price for Bulletproof Coffee versus the competitors says that the person is a high performer. On the other hand, drinking Black Rifle Coffee, which we mentioned earlier, says you shoot guns, or that you don't care about the opinions of other people. The product (coffee) is almost exactly the same, but the *person* is completely different.

Compare that to one of my friends, James.

James was a sportscaster on ESPN who left his job to become an entrepreneur. For several years, he wondered what type of business to start, until he started listening to my podcast. One day, he was running on the beach while listening to me outline the path to a million dollars (the same process you're discovering right now, by the way). He stopped mid-run. "I think I can do this," he said.

James had previously struggled with sleeping at night until he discovered the source of his challenges—the light from being on his computer late at night was causing insomnia. James found the solution in wearing blue-blocker glasses, which filter high-energy visible (HEV) blue light, when he was on the computer before bedtime. They helped him sleep, but they were ugly as all get-out. Pain point alert!

So James developed the solution. He decided to make glasses with the same blue-blocking function that didn't make the wearer look like a dork. He noticed that competitors were selling blue-blocking glasses for about $8 a pair. Most people would balk at the low profit margins, but James created a brand that was specifically for insomnia sufferers. That allowed him to charge a higher price and have the profit margin needed to create a great product.

The product did extremely well. Customers loved it, and he built a brand that people were proud to show off. However, the company ran into a challenge: What does it sell next?

Its next product was a different style of blue-blocker glasses, and it bombed. What happened?

Well, James had bought into the belief that he was selling glasses, not helping people with sleep problems. He had focused on the product, not the person. He needed to discover that he was a sleep company, not a glasses company. Once that was solved, it was easy to come up with three to five new products that the company could sell. That changes everything.

It's tempting to fall into the trap that your business sells products, because that's where the money comes from. But products are bought by *people*, and you must know who they are if you want to hit a million dollars.

The Foundational Questions

When my friends hear about my students' successes, they often reach out and ask to "pick my brain." In most cases, they have a series of questions before they feel comfortable taking action.

Two of my friends, Carly and Carly (yup), invited me over for lunch one day. They were setting out to be entrepreneurs, and they needed help clarifying their first steps. As soon as I was done chewing, they started firing questions at me (this happens a lot; I'm used to it).

When it came down to it, every question in the barrage they threw at me amounted to: *What business should we start?*

I went through a few options with them, and, by dessert, they had a solid idea that they were really excited about. When I left, I knew they were on a good path with a clear direction. The next time they invited me over for lunch, they wanted to update me on their progress. I couldn't wait to hear how their new business was going.

As soon as I got there, however, question hour resumed: "Ryan, what business should we *really* start?" Here we were, back to square one.

They had no prototype, no audience, and no proof of concept. They'd been stuck spinning in place because they were waiting to be told what to do. What I helped them discover was that there was no perfect product or "right" business to start. Instead, there's simply a set of decisions you need to make.

Once you make these decisions, you'll have a good shot at success. But until you make these decisions, you'll be stuck in analysis mode forever. Again, you don't need to know how to do anything—we'll go into more detail on the process throughout the rest of this book.

First, you must make decisions. It's also okay to *change* your decisions later, but answering these questions will allow you to start to move down the path to your own million-dollar business.

1. To whom are you going to sell? You start by identifying your person. It can be you or someone you know, but once you identify them, look at what group of people they belong to. Are they CrossFitters? Do they eat a paleo diet? Are they nurses? Are they Christians? If you don't know the answer, start with yourself. What groups do *you* identify with?

2. What do they already buy? Can you list at least three to five products that your group already buys? If you can't list at least three products, you're in the wrong market. At this point in the process, it's really tempting to make up a product idea from scratch, but I recommend that you start by identifying what your person already buys. Just start writing down what your person already buys on their journey to be a great mom, a great entrepreneur, or a great designer.

3. Which product out of that suite of products do you want to focus on, to either make a great version of it or a version that solves one of their problems? Looking at the list of products you came up with, ask yourself, "How are those products *not* serving my group right now?" Does one of them jump out as a potential "gateway" to the rest of the list? If you identify the first product that solves a pain point or serves as a gateway into other purchases, then you know exactly where to start.

4. What does your group think about similar products on the market? If you have a group of products you're thinking about focusing on, you can start to identify "holes" in the marketplace by listening to what people are already saying. Read customer reviews and look at internet forums. You can also start vetting your idea by posting about it online. My buddy Moiz tried using Tom's natural deodorant, and he hated it for a simple reason: It didn't work. He thought, *I wonder if I could do this better.* So he started asking questions on online forums, getting feedback from other natural yuppies like him. From the response, he knew there was interest. He did a $500 round of prototypes and sold out immediately. That was the beginning of Native Deodorant, which was later acquired by Procter & Gamble for $100 million. It took Moiz only eighteen months to go from a $500 prototype to a million-dollar brand (and it sold for *nine* figures!).

5. Where does your person hang out with others? With an idea of what we *might* sell, we can start to think about where our first customers *might* come from. It's much easier to make sales when you can drop your product in front of a group of your ideal people. Does your target customer listen to specific podcasts? Do they follow certain influencers? Do they belong to specific groups? Do they read certain blogs? Brainstorm where your ideal customer focuses his or her *attention*, and you will quickly know where to put your product in front of them. In the next chapters, you will also learn how to develop a micro-audience that is ready to buy your product from you. I also like to write down the names of ten friends who will get excited about a product because your ideal customers know other people just like them.

6. Do you know how you will get predictable sales? I don't mean to overwhelm you just yet, but your sales process has to be scalable. For most people, Amazon is the easiest place to start. We'll cover that later. Unless you have a different way to collect sales consistently, then Amazon will be your starting place.

7. What will be products two, three, and four? Do you know what your follow-up products are going to be? If you don't know what else you might sell to your person, then you're not ready to move on. Your job will be to roll out products for that same customer as quickly as possible and as fast as you can comfortably handle them for the first year. Having an idea of your subsequent products will put you far ahead in the process.

When Matt and I started Sheer Strength, we went through the same process, and asked ourselves the same questions I'm asking you.

We knew our group because we *were* our group. And we knew that people in our group bought protein powder, creatine, and pre-workout and post-workout products. We bought workout bands, BCAAs, drinks, gym memberships, and workout clothes. We identified our gateway product and brainstormed the rest of the list. Other companies were successfully selling similar products, and most people probably would have avoided that market because of the competition. But those other companies had done a bunch of research and development for us. They'd already vetted the idea and shown that people were buying the product.

Matt knew the names of a couple manufacturers, so we emailed them and ordered samples for our gateway product—an endurance supplement. The samples were all fine, but they were boring and mostly the same; this was our chance to add our unique spin. We wanted to add in one ingredient: beetroot extract. We'd done some research and found that it was particularly helpful for endurance. When we tried it, it made a massive difference for us—and nobody else was putting it into their formulas yet. Today, beetroot is a common ingredient in similar products, probably because we pioneered it.

However, we knew that we didn't want to be just an "endurance supplement" company. Since we were developing the products *we* wanted, we made a long list of other products we would eventually want to sell. If the first product took off, we'd know exactly what we could sell next.

Our first product sold okay, but it was nothing special out of the gate. It took months to get to about twenty-five sales per day, and that's when we rolled out the next line of products. Remember, it only takes three to five products that each sells about twenty-five sales per day. That's a million-dollar business.

Having ideas circling around in your brain right now is a really good sign you're ready to move forward. If you're not there yet, it would be a good idea to answer the list of foundational questions (see page 36).

But anyone can sit and "kick around ideas" all day. That's the easy part.

The hard part is deciding to take the risk of actually bringing that product to life. The hardest part is getting past the head noise: *What will my family think? What if my product sucks? What if I get a negative review?*

While I will help you with the "how to," you have to go all in on getting through the mental hurdles.

It's time to make a decision: Are you willing to go all in?

Entrepreneur Spotlight: Jared Springer

When Jared Springer stumbled across my training for entrepreneurs, he was at a low spot in his life. Recently born with clubbed feet, his son had terrible medical issues, which put Jared in a lot of debt. Then, to compound things, Jared started developing his own medical problems.

One day, he was rushed to the emergency room unable to walk. Apparently, a large nerve running down his leg was completely pinched. Doctors told him, "You either have emergency surgery, or you never walk again."

At the time, Jared, who was thirty years old and married with two small kids, worked in management and sales. Suddenly he found himself in a walker with a long road to recovery ahead of him. This was when Jared came across my videos. Having plenty of time on his hands, he watched every single piece of content I put out. Then he did all the action steps.

Jared was fired up to launch a business. There was one major problem: He didn't have the money to start a company. He was still in recovery, in debt, and unable to work. He had to hustle and grind his way to success. He started flipping random products to get enough money to invest in his business. Once he had a little bit of capital, he developed his first product.

In the end, his first product was a failure. Instead of giving up, though, Jared went back to basics and began building a Facebook following—he focused on the *person*, and he got them to follow his page, which ultimately swelled to 60,000 followers, adding some of them to an email list, as well. That's when he started testing out different products.

Just before Christmas, he found a little robotic dog bank in which you put a quarter in its mouth and it chomps down on it. Right away, he knew: *I can sell that!* He knew his person so well that he knew that this off-the-wall product would be successful.

Prior to this, his business had been struggling, operating in the red. But when he talked about his product on Facebook, it caught on, and things started to take off. Orders began coming in quickly—so quickly that his orders exceeded his inventory, and he had to start taking pre-orders. He wired $40,000 to a supplier in China for additional product—up until recently, that had been a year's income for him! (As I tell people over and over again, when you follow the process, your biggest problem won't be a lack of sales, but possibly *too many* sales!)

Then the unimaginable happened: His inventory order got tied up in customs for two weeks. He'd originally had plenty of time until Christmas; he'd even paid for the shipping to be expedited via air freight. But now none of his orders would be fulfilled in time.

He threw a Hail Mary, called the manager at FedEx customs, and told her that if it wasn't on a truck the next day he would be bankrupt. Incredibly, this worked. She got the shipment on a truck that night.

Even so, Jared was running out of time. If he didn't get people their orders, he would have to refund their money—but he had spent all of the money on advertising and ordering the product. There was no money for refunds. It was a week before Christmas, and he had 5,000 orders to ship. Each item had to be quickly boxed and shipped to reach its destination on time. Since there was no time to send them to a fulfillment warehouse, he had to do it himself.

So Jared had thousands of units shipped to his house in the middle of winter in Wisconsin. He stayed awake for days printing labels and organizing shipments. The FedEx truck backed up to his house and dropped the pallets in the middle of the driveway, just as a snowstorm was about to hit. Jared and fifteen friends frantically packaged and labeled them in just six hours, right up until the moment they were picked up to ship to their destinations.

It was Jared's mindset, his willingness to grind in the early days of his company, that kept him going—failure was not an option.

In the end, Jared made a couple hundred thousand dollars in a few short months that Christmas. It was the first product to launch the Happy Puppin brand into profitability. One year later, the brand had brought in a million dollars in revenue. Now Happy Puppin is a seven-figure operation that's currently about to be sold for a big payday.

"Most people think you need tens of thousands of dollars to get started, but you can get there with just a thousand, or less," Jared told me. "The money isn't the obstacle. The truth is that ninety percent of the battle is getting your head right and just pushing through all the obstacles, no matter what. You have to make it your mission to find a way."

Jared's obstacles didn't end that sleepless Christmas. To this day, competitors copy his ads, and even his products. Some of them are total scam artists who take orders with no intention of fulfilling them.

"When I first started, I'd get so angry at the scammers, but that wasn't helping me," he said. "Now, if I see someone copying my stuff, I immediately get my lawyers involved and send a cease and desist. It's part of the game. I've learned to just deal with it."

To Jared, being an entrepreneur is an up-and-down emotional roller coaster. "You have to get your mindset right," he said. "You'll have really big wins, you'll be doing awesome, and then something turns on a dime and knocks you back down. You have to train your mind to make those peaks less dramatic, so you can flow through it."

This was Jared's biggest struggle. For a while, he was either on top of the world or he felt like everything was falling down around him. Once he built up the mental fortitude to realize that there would always be ups and downs, it all got easier.

The moment Jared really knew he'd made it was when he bought a brand-new truck—a Ram Rebel with huge 33-inch tires—and took his family on a month-long vacation.

"At that moment, I felt like it all became real," Jared said. "All the hard work and grind had given me the kind of freedom I'd always wanted. I remember thinking, *This thing really works!*"

4

Step Two:
Develop Your First Product

When Moiz Ali, founder of Native Deodorant, started the business, he put in a grand total of $500. Two years later, he sold the company to Procter & Gamble for $100 million.

That's a pretty good return on investment, I'd say.

"We bootstrapped the whole thing," Moiz said from the stage of one of our conferences. "We launched on Product Hunt, and the most entrepreneurial of entrepreneurs go on this site and upvote and downvote it on a daily basis. On day one, we'd sold one bar and were at the very bottom of the list on Product Hunt. *Forget it,* I said, *I'm shutting this business down.*"

Then a friend of his said he had an "in" at Product Hunt and that he could get Native near the top. By the next day, they'd sold fifty bars and were at the top of the list.

"Once we had those first fifty orders, we bought our first hundred units," said Moiz. "We sold the first fifty bars without even having any inventory. If you bought on a Tuesday, your product was made within one day of the order. We had zero inventory laying around, and it allowed us to stay really lean."

Moiz didn't use Amazon, retail, or Kickstarter. He sent all traffic to one place, the company website, and encouraged visitors to subscribe to its email list in exchange for a $2 discount. People usually subscribed, which increased Native's conversion rate.

"When we tested this, we kept the test going a good six weeks past the planned duration, even though we already had hard data that it definitely worked, that people subscribed and that subscribers were more likely to become customers," said Moiz. "The reason was that I was certain in my heart of hearts that it shouldn't be so. But that's the thing—when it comes to marketing, I have no idea. Despite spending all the money we've spent on ads and all the success we've had with creative, I still don't know what's going to work. I'm not the customer. That's why we test *everything*."

While Native is based in San Francisco, it didn't raise capital like everyone in Silicon Valley. Instead, it tested its products like tech companies test software, according to Moiz. "Early on, when we launched in 2015, we realized we had a pretty mediocre repurchase rate—twenty percent. Our reviews were coming in at an average of four stars. We started simply asking customers why they didn't buy it again. *You were willing to spend twelve dollars on this deodorant; why didn't you buy it again?*"

The answer, Moiz found, was resoundingly *application*; customers didn't like how the deodorant applied. It was too flaky. They spent the entire first year of the business working to solve that problem. They were also focused on staining; Moiz would A/B test products by rubbing them on all his shirts, throwing them in the wash, and seeing what happened. With all the testing the company did, it was ready to launch a reformulated product in a year.

The new formulation was "infinitely superior" to the original. Reviews went from 4 stars to 4.7 stars, and repeat purchases doubled.

It's easy to fall prey to "shiny object syndrome" and lose your priorities, Moiz cautioned. "One of our investors told us we needed to launch into other categories, and that no one was going to buy a single-category business. But I felt that things were going so well that I didn't want to lose my focus on it. If I branch into another business category, what are the chances I'd be able to do it as well as this business is going? Our sales channels were also questioned—we were approached by Target, Whole Foods, Costco, Sephora, Ulta. The number of brick-and-mortar stores that approached us was a hundred pages long. We decided to stay laser-focused on what we were good at—selling on our website—because what we were doing was working. We doubled down on what was working, instead of getting bogged down by the typical dogma of other startups in Silicon Valley.

"We didn't do *any* influencer marketing for years. People told us we were crazy. You don't have to listen to all of the noise out there. Whatever your team is doing well that's generating revenue, double down on it. Stay focused on what you're doing well and ignore everything else."

When it was time to go to market, Moiz knew he'd grown an immensely profitable business, but to a point. He felt confident that he could build from nothing into an eight-figure business. But he didn't feel confident he could build a $100 million business. He wasn't sure he had the skill set to take the business to the next level, of playing with the big boys. The initial acquisition conversation was actually *not* with Procter & Gamble, its eventual buyers; it was with another business that came knocking on Moiz's door and wanted to talk "partnering" (which always means "buying"). Valuation conversations started happening, and Moiz quickly realized that he needed to run a real process and do it right. He made a list of a hundred companies he might want to sell to, crossed out all the companies he didn't like, and ended up with a list of sixteen people to go talk to.

"And we did just that, talked to those sixteen people," he told us. "We'd give our presentation and show off our business. We ended up just really falling in love with the folks at Procter & Gamble."

Proctor & Gamble loved them back—so much so that they bought the company for a cool $100 million.

You always start small. But when you focus on what works, you get incredible results.

How to Make Your First Product

When I was six, my aunt had a boyfriend named Don.

Don was the first rich person I ever met. To this day, I don't know how Don made his money; I just remember the one time he blew my mind.

We were sitting on my parents' front porch, and he was giving me my first "business lesson." I had asked him to teach me about being successful. (Yes, at six years old. When you're a real entrepreneur, you're born with the itch.)

Don's first lesson to me was on product creation. To this day, I remember it clearly: "Ryan, did you know there are companies out there that can make any idea you have come to life?"

"What do you mean?" I asked.

"What's something that you and your friends are interested in right now?"

"Yo-yos," I said. "At recess all my friends bring their yo-yos out and compare tricks."

"What's one of the tricks called?"

"Walk-the-dog."

"If you wanted to come up with a yo-yo that would bark when you do walk-the-dog, you could call one of these companies, and they could make that happen and send it to you."

I could barely believe it. Companies could do that? Imagine how impressed my friends would be if I showed up next recess with a barking yo-yo!

I now know that Don was talking about *contract manufacturers*—companies that make your product for you and sell it to you at wholesale. However, much to my great childhood remorse, Don didn't actually know how to find these companies.

Twenty years later, I discovered that Don was right. Other people will bring your ideas to life, and if you like it, you can order it in small (or large) quantities. It really can be that easy to take a gateway *idea* and make it a gateway *product*. Thankfully, today you don't need to "know someone" to have a product made, as contract manufacturers compete for your business online.

You'll find a ton of contract manufacturers if you search for them on Google, but the biggest marketplace in the world is Alibaba.com, where you can shop contract manufacturers to find the product you want to create.

Don's lesson was top-of-mind when I started my second brand with my buddy Sean. Sean and I were good partners because we filled gaps in each other's game. I was in charge of decisions and marketing, and Sean was in charge of research and operations. When we were trying to identify our target customer, he spent a ton of time putting together spreadsheets comparing all the different markets we should consider.

When he showed them to me and asked me what I thought, I replied, "Yoga."

Huh? "We could easily do multiple products serving people who do yoga," I told him. "It's an emerging trend. And I know a ton of those people; I can ask them what they want. Let's start a yoga business."

Sean's initial response was, "*That's not a quantitative analysis, Ryan!*" I've never been one to overthink things—most people spend way too much time in the research period. I make decisions fast and adjust later.

With our target customer identified, we made a list of possible products and chose our gateway product—a yoga mat. With that, we began the process of product development. We looked up the top-selling yoga mats on Amazon and read through the reviews; we asked questions on Facebook groups, subreddits, and Instagram influencer accounts. It didn't take long before we had an idea of the main pain points we needed to address with our first product.

I remembered Don's advice and began looking for people to make the product.

With a quick scroll and a click, we could choose between a wholesaler in China, a private label supplier out of India, or a contract manufacturer in Vietnam. For about fifty bucks, we were able to order a set of yoga mat samples that had the exact features we were looking for. It was that easy.

Samples in hand, we needed to refine our product idea to make sure we were really hitting the pain points we'd identified. At that time, I'd done yoga maybe two or three times in my life, and I wasn't nearly the right demographic for our mats anyway. That forced me to ask questions.

We were targeting yoga-loving millennials, so I went where they often congregate: Starbucks. There, I did the kind of tough field work that really makes an entrepreneur sweat: asking young women questions over coffee.

"Which yoga mat do you prefer? Why?"

"What makes the difference between a bad yoga mat and a good one?"

"What's wrong with your current yoga mat?"

"What do you think of this one? And what about this one?"

Next, I headed over to local yoga studios to see how our samples stacked up against the strenuous demands of a yoga class. A few classes later, Sean and I had everything we needed to narrow down our product development.

Armed with all our data, we went back to the manufacturers. From a couple yoga-clueless guys, we'd become knowledgeable enough to know not just what a good yoga mat looked like, but how it had to feel and perform. We knew what we needed *our* yoga mat to *do*. Now we just had to find the manufacturer to supply it.

It didn't take long to find some willing partners. We set down the specifications, and Sean talked to all the manufacturers who said they could fulfill our requests. We narrowed it down to two quality options, and then we choose the one with the best price and the best communication. Sean ordered the prototype, had it embossed with our brand logo—Zen Active—and in no time at all, we unrolled our first yoga mat on the floor in Sean's house.

That was *our* yoga mat. It was our product, with our specifications, with our logo, in Sean's house, ready for sale. And all it took was one website and a lot of groundwork asking questions.

Now, I'm not saying we got the product totally right on our first try. We made some mistakes, and we made adjustments to improve the product over time, but the basics of taking an idea and making it a ready-for-market product really is this simple. All you have to do is find the suppliers, do the research, make the tweaks, and find the best offer out there.

Find Your Supplier

I've come to trust and rely on suppliers from Alibaba.com, but I know it has its detractors. When it comes to user experience, the site is, frankly, a bit of a mess. There's also a certain distance between you and the supplier that the more firm-handshake-loving, look-them-in-the-eye-while-you're-negotiating types don't like.

These days, though, Alibaba has a lot of competition, so there are plenty of options out there if you want a different path to your product. You can search for wholesalers, manufacturing companies, or contract manufacturers for your chosen product and find any number of smaller companies you can contact personally to get that more direct experience.

Or, if you're feeling particularly old-fashioned, you can attend a trade show in the market you're going into. Find out where the next event is, hop on a plane, and go speak to a room full of potential manufacturers in a new city. Some people even go so far as to fly to China to meet directly with manufacturers. I've never done that—and I never plan to do that—but plenty of my friends swear by it.

Of these options, though, I'd still recommend starting on Alibaba or a similar site and ordering ready-made product samples. Something magical happens when you hold a product in your hand: You realize it's *real*.

While it may seem at the outset like the best way to make your perfect product is to go meet a contract manufacturer in person and get them to build your design from scratch, that option comes with a lot more risk: the risk of *lost time*. We're talking about at least three months before you see your first prototype—more likely six, or even twelve. All of that and you won't even know right away if the resulting prototype will be *the one* that will make your brand. That's why I recommend you come up with the idea, get samples, and improve over time.

Perfectionists hate the approach, but you can't expect to make it to a million dollars in twelve months if it takes twelve months just to get a look at what you're creating.

Refine It; Don't Overthink It

A lot of entrepreneurs think that success in business requires you to reinvent the wheel, and that you have to reinvent it *perfectly* the first time. If you don't have a wheel that can do something new from the moment you debut it, no one's ever going to bother buying it, right? It's got to be new, and it's got to be perfect, and until you've got that down, best keep it to yourself.

That may have been true at some point in the past, but it certainly isn't now. The wheel hasn't been reinvented in ages—and yet wheel manufacturers and wheel dealers are doing just fine. In fact, new wheel competitors still pop up every now and again. What are they selling? The same damn wheels, just tweaked.

The key to your product probably won't be that it's new. It'll be that it's *different*, even if it's just in one small way.

Here's what I mean: I was once the keynote speaker at a conference where an attendee came up and told me she was marketing yoga classes to baby boomers. After a little while, she mentioned that her client group's biggest challenge was knee pain when they got on a yoga mat. The majority of yoga mats are manufactured and marketed toward young people.

You can turn that information into a great product in two ways. You can either design a new, extra-thick yoga mat made out of a new material that no one has ever thought to try before. Or, you can take an extra-thick yoga mat that already exists, and focus on speaking to a new customer: boomers who do yoga.

Don't waste time trying to come up with a new wheel—simply give your person what they already want. Once you have some samples in hand, focus on refining, not revolutionizing. I know the temptation is to pursue perfection, but perfect doesn't sell. That's not to say that quality and uniqueness don't sell—they do—but sales *force you to improve the quality of the product.* As Peter Diamandis says, "If you are not embarrassed by the first iteration of your product, then you aren't moving fast enough."

Instead of trying to think yourself to success, focus on getting more feedback on your samples, so that you can refine what isn't working, and really target those who will be receptive to your product.

In this work, you've got to focus on the big decisions first and worry about everything else later. Address a pain point with your product, reach out to those who have that problem, and then get feedback (preferably in the form of sales). The longer you search for the ideal product or the ideal branding, the longer your product lives in fairy-dust land rather than in a reality where it can secure you that financial freedom.

I've known far too many people who get hung up on designing packaging when they should be getting their product ready to sell. They work and rework a logo, change out the color of their plastic wrapping, consider a hundred different fonts for their brand name. Honestly, if you're selling a product on Amazon, most people won't even notice your packaging. For the customer, the packaging is a brown Amazon box on the doorstep. If the product speaks to them, they'll get it regardless of the plastic you wrap it in.

I don't want to give the impression that design features aren't important at all. The branding, the logo, the overall design—that's all going to be important in expanding your reach. But you can change that later. The only things you can't change later are the things that prevent you from taking a sale in the first place.

Your job now is to eliminate all those things as quickly as possible. Concentrate on getting the research done, so you can get the product right, go to market, and start taking sales. If the packaging isn't up to your dreamed-up standards, come back to it after you're moving inventory and money is flowing into your bank account.

Refining your product is a never-ending process. When we first started selling yoga mats, my attention was solely on moving those first products. Shortly after we'd gone up on Amazon, though, we found a more affordable manufacturer whose mats were thicker, higher quality, and a dollar less per unit. A better deal for a better product was out there, but I didn't put our momentum on hold to look for it. We made the adjustment as we progressed. That never-ending, purpose-driven quest for improvement gives you the freedom to direct your focus right now on getting that product on the market.

Whenever I catch myself overthinking a product and delaying the crucial move from concept to sale, I remind myself, "Let's make some mistakes." After all, there's so *little* risk involved in this method; when you're working with small orders up front, the downside of a mistake is very low. You'll find a way to sell those first 100 units on Amazon eventually. Even if you don't, the loss is minimal.

Mistakes, even bad ones, are a part of this business. No amount of preparation ensures a perfect process. Sometimes you'll make a modest mistake, like going to market with the second-best supplier cutting slightly into your margins.

Other times, you'll commit a nastier error, like the time we lowered the price on our yoga mats without really thinking through our inventory limitations.

At that point, we were still in the small order phase, hedging our bets with a limited supply of yoga mats. Up to that point, we'd kept the price high, which was great. Profit margins were solid. We were attracting the right people. We had a steady but not overwhelming number of sales.

Then we decided we wanted to chase a higher Amazon ranking. A better ranking would mean more eyes on the product and more purchases; it seemed a nice shortcut to upgrading to larger orders and bigger profits. To do that, though, we needed to boost sales. So we slashed the price, handing out a better bargain to the customer.

A lot of beginner entrepreneurs—and a fair number of experienced ones, too—are afraid of high prices. They want to cut prices as soon as financially possible, probably because some intro-to-business class told them that's the best way to build a brand. I can tell you from experience, though, that if you're building a brand, you don't want to get into the business of cutting prices. You want to be near the top price point in your market.

The reason is simple: It's much easier to scale a premium brand than it is to scale a low-priced brand. Only companies selling inventory in massive quantities can really win at that game. You're not going to beat Walmart's price, so don't play Walmart's game.

When we cut our price, we sold really well (because when you follow the method in this book, it works), but we ran out of stock. It was a predictable outcome. Being out of stock is the *worst* thing that can possibly happen to your new business because you're essentially out of business when you can't take orders.

We had to wait out the four-week lag for another shipment to cross an ocean and get to the Amazon warehouse. When we finally got new stock back in, we were essentially starting over. Yes, we had customer reviews, but our momentum was dead. We had to run another discount to get moving again. We did recover, but that one mistake set us back months.

I can't say whether an extra month of planning would have kept us from making that awful choice; probably not, honestly. You can't control for everything. Your goal is just to take your product from an *idea* to a physical item in a customer's hand.

It's simpler than most people think it is. Find the right supplier, get samples, refine with research, put in a small order, and get the product online. That's all you need to worry about right now. Don't overthink it. Just fix the mistakes as they come.

One of my mastermind members, Travis Killian, once told me about how he gets products to stand out in a busy, loud marketplace. His answer was simple: "We listen to people. We execute so many split tests, it's insane. We'll mock up the product and ask people, *Which do you like better? This one or this other one from our competitor?* We do that for all the top competitors in the market, all the ones we think have the best products in the niche."

Split testing requires nothing more than asking people which one of two things they like better. That's it. Show someone two items, and ask for his or her preference. It's one of those rare things that happens to be simple, easy, *and* effective.

"I remember one time, when we were just starting out," Travis told me, "we paid one of our friends to go to the mall in Austin, show pictures of our products versus our competitor's products, and collect survey answers on which one they preferred."

If it sounds like a ton of time and money to pay someone to do in-person surveys and split testing, Travis says that's not even essential. "When we started out, that's what we did. Now, we use services online to run constant split tests of our products against our competitors' products. The most important thing is to get the feedback on *why* survey respondents have a preference. Why do they like the other guy's product over mine? That's the data we really want to collect. We spend our time analyzing that data and applying it to the products—deciding first if the feedback is something we can, and want, to address, and then making changes from there."

All of this happens *before* the product is released to the market.

"Say you use a French press to make coffee," said Travis. "There are tons of French press designs out there—some are full stainless steel, some have mostly glass, some are more sleek, curved designs, some are more industrial. What we'd do to develop and split test a French press is collect all the product designs we think are best and then split test them against the top sellers in the category. Based on the split test, we'll decide on which design to go with."

Getting customer feedback is a direct result of getting sales, according to Travis. "When you launch a product, you do whatever you can to get as many sales as you can early on, because that's what drives feedback. That's what allows you to listen to your customer. When we first started out, we went from, in four months, doing four to five thousand in sales a month, to two years in, doing about two million in sales a month."

Those sales are the fuel that runs the feedback machine and allows new products to be developed.

Moving Beyond Small-Time

It's normal to feel nervous or downright terrified to place an inventory order, especially when you don't know if the product is going to sell. You can mitigate that fear by listening closely to your person, and also using the "Stacking the Deck" strategies I'll outline in later chapters. However, it's okay to start small. You might only order 100 units of a product when you start. That's what I did.

However, once you start to see sales, all your attention is going to go into *keeping enough product*. That will require you to place larger inventory orders. Getting to the point where you're financed enough to make that transition can be tricky. In other words, managing the money side of this can be a challenge for first-time entrepreneurs.

It's counterintuitive, but your goal at the beginning isn't to maximize profit; your goal at this stage of the process is to establish the systems of getting product and selling it. You will optimize for profit later.

A student of mine who was selling a fish oil supplement kept trying to find a way around the upgrade cost by switching suppliers. He was constantly looking to improve his supply chain process, jumping from supplier to supplier as soon as one would offer a slightly better price.

His margins did improve modestly every time, but the supply chain wasn't predictable. He kept running out of product—which, again, is the *worst* thing that can happen to your business. Instead of progress, he was circling around the same difficulty, making small orders, jumping to another supplier, making another small order, and then promptly running out of stock. Margins don't mean anything when you can't guarantee you'll have the product people want when they want to buy it. What's more, he was missing out on building the necessary momentum to cover expansion.

When he came to me for advice, I told him he had to learn to stay put with someone and make it work. The solution to his problem was to settle into a deeper relationship with a supplier.

"Which supplier?"

"If all your suppliers seem about equal in price and quality," I told him, "choose the one with the best communication."

So he went out to New York City and met one supplier face-to-face, then used that strong communication to negotiate better terms. He got a 20 percent discount on his product, a 20 percent boost to his profits, and the consistency to keep the product moving without interruption.

For him, making the jump to larger orders in the hundreds of units was as easy as sitting down with the right manufacturer and making a great deal. He had the supply, he had the demand, and he had the margins to make it work.

Not everyone is that lucky. For the rest of us, getting product made and sold introduces a new problem: funding.

To scale past small-time operations, and to make sure you always have the inventory on hand to meet increasing demand—to make it to the million—you will probably face a money problem. That problem cripples many new entrepreneurs, but if you play your hand right, it can help you grow even faster.

Entrepreneur Spotlight: Hanny Sunarto

Hanny Sunarto, an engineer who lives in Illinois, is originally from Indonesia. Once a year, she makes the long trip to visit her family.

She and her sister have always used this opportunity to go on a two- to three-week hiking and travel adventure. The sisters were out in the wild in 2015 when one of their backpacks broke.

Frustrated, Hanny's sister asked her, "You're an engineer, right? Why don't you design a better backpack?"

It may have started as a joke, but the idea stuck with Hanny. By the end of the trip, she had the concept for her company, NeatPack.

Hanny started working on designs. Her sister, who frequently traveled to China for her fashion and textile business, looked for the right textiles and other materials for their first product. The company's target audience was minimalist travelers looking for affordable, high-quality travel bags, as opposed to high-end leather luggage. The bags would do two things really well: organize all your travel items and never, ever break.

Hanny's attention to detail and her "all in" mentality is what persuaded me to invest in her business once it started to take sales. However, she had to overcome her own set of challenges, just as everyone does.

The sisters' first product was a toiletry bag with an adjustable compartment, a small interior unit you could set your toothpaste in without having it turn into a mess. Hanny started with just a sketch of the underlying concept, an approach she was accustomed to from her work as an engineer. Her sister found a supplier who was also helpful in fleshing out a 3-D design using AutoCAD. The sketch became a blueprint, and the sisters and supplier iterated on the design until it was right.

This first product only took a couple iterations to get the product to a stage where the commitment for a minimum order of a thousand units could be made. The concept originated in June or July 2015, and the company launched its first product in late November. By that time, Hanny's husband had come aboard to help out.

The response from their audience was almost immediately positive. Hanny already belonged to several Facebook travel groups, so the sisters set up and launched a new travel group of their own. "My sister and I came up with this great new design for a travel toiletry bag," they said.

They got a lot of "Wow, that's pretty cool" responses, to which they followed up with, "It's going to be on Amazon in a couple of weeks if you want to check it out."

Members of the Facebook group started posting on social media, saying how much they loved the new toiletry bag. That's when the sisters finally knew their design was legit.

When NeatPack launched its second product, Hanny and her sister thought it was the greatest thing in the world. It flopped. Customers said that the material wasn't light or flexible enough, that it was hard to fold into a backpack or suitcase, and that it was too large. Although the design underwent a fair amount of tweaking, the product was eventually discontinued.

This was an ego-bruising disappointment, of course. Hanny felt she knew what she was doing. After all, she's both an engineer and intrepid traveler. She and her sister came up with all sorts of justifications for why their products were superior. Unfortunately, market response didn't bear them out.

Hanny has seen many other sellers get similarly carried away, wasting far too much money on an unproven concept. They're so sure they've got a hit on their hands that they launch in five different channels right away. *It's going to work. People will love it.*

You only know that once you get feedback, sales, or both. Focus on proof of concept for one product sold through a single channel.

Make sure it's what your audience needs and wants and get as much feedback as you can as early as possible.

How many times Hanny, her sister, and her husband would go back to the drawing board during the design phase was determined on a product-by-product basis. The company developed a mailing list from its Facebook group and other travel groups and continually asked for feedback. Customers listed pros and cons and also gave the company ideas for future products.

Through it all, though, they felt incredibly lucky to have an audience who gave honest feedback and felt like a community. They knew right away if products weren't liked or had to be returned, and in a couple of cases, they made the decision to cut their losses and discontinue an item.

The company's first toiletry bag was compact in size; customers soon began asking for a bigger toiletry bag that could be used for the family and kids. This medium-sized toiletry bag was developed and launched in about seven months and was the company's second major success. Subsequent successes included a sling bag, which is now one of the company's best sellers, a foldable backpack, and a cross-body bag for women.

Hanny believes one of her company's major early mistakes was putting too much focus on selling through Amazon, losing the more important focus on brand-building as a result. Growth stalled in 2016 because not enough attention had been paid to defining, creating, and expanding the brand's core audience.

In 2017, to overcome this setback, NeatPack hired a marketing agency to help expand its mailing list. The resulting increased exposure and series of promotions grew the customer base from 3,000 to 10,000 and created a major boost in subsequent product launches. Leveraging the mailing list enabled the company to launch its cross-body bag profitably right off the bat.

"If you're thinking of starting a business . . . you have to remember that proof of concept is key," Hanny says. "I've seen a lot of people fail because they were spinning their wheels on less critical aspects of the business. Go ahead and sell your product on Amazon, your website, or whatever your preferred channel may be, but get a proof of concept first, before a lot of money is spent unnecessarily. Is your product something the market, and your audience, really needs?"

That kind of focus is what led me to invest in Hanny a few years ago, and while I may have bought into her company, I was really buying into *her*.

5

Step Three:
Funding Your Business

Plenty of companies start out with a bang.

It often doesn't last long. Frequently, companies will launch with a huge push, or a great viral marketing campaign that sticks them in customers' minds—but the stickiness is only so strong. Within months or a year, that initial spike of sales and attention ends.

The companies that stick around are those that can comfortably handle their own growth.

Earlier, we discussed Dollar Shave Club, and how it grew toward a billion-dollar exit. What most people don't know about Dollar Shave Club is that it was started on a shoestring budget. Dubin sold excess razor inventory, and it was enough to develop a real customer base. And the famous "our razors are fucking great" video cost just $5,000 to produce.

"I bootstrapped it for the first year, and then I raised a first round of $100,000 in January 2012," Michael said. "That seeded the growth that happened in 2012. Then the viral video hit in March of 2012."

Dubin said he floated out of the meeting, excited to secure $100,000 in funding. It was a vote of confidence in his ability to be an entrepreneur. He invested the money into customer acquisition, which paved the way for their now-famous viral video. The viral video brought in enough customers to create a steady drumbeat of new sales, which allowed the company to keep investing into growth. The viral sensation of that original video wore off, but the company had built a stream of creative media to keep them front and center in customers' attention spans.

As the company grew, Dubin continued to double down on putting money into advertising to acquire new customers, rather than staying married to one way of doing things. "At Dollar Shave Club, we used a combination of television, radio, display ads, and Facebook ads, and made sure that our prospective customers got a very precisely number of touches on the brand in order to convert them," he said.

Still, he recommended testing small: "If you're a young company, think about local media. It's a great way to get a blend of attention on a cost scale you can afford. And you'll see how different media nourish customer growth in different ways."

There was one burning question that I had to know. "You turned $100,000 into a billion. Were your investors happy with their return on investment?" I joked.

"They were," he quipped.

You may not raise $100,000 like Dubin, but the good news is that you don't need to, especially at the start. Michael didn't raise any money until he had proven sales. Most of the entrepreneurs I know get sales *first*, and then they consider outside capital.

Should you go looking outside your own bank account for money, being able to show off your ability to hook new customers will be your calling card for investors. By the time you finish reading this book, "getting customers" will be the easy part, and keeping up with growth will be your biggest challenge.

More Sales Does Not Equal More Profit

My first product order for Sheer Strength cost me $600. I ordered 100 units at $6 each and we sold it at a $32 price point. The money came out of my savings, and at the time, I was *so* worried that it wouldn't sell, and I'd be out $600.

To the Ryan of the past, I now say two things.

First: Who cares? Put on your big boy pants, Ryan. It's only $600.

Second: This isn't the real problem. Assuming you follow this process, create a decent product, and identify your customer, your bigger problem is that you won't be able to keep inventory in stock, as we've talked about already. Trust me on this. Keeping inventory in stock so that you can keep building your sales momentum is a real challenge.

With Sheer Strength, we kept raising the price until it hit a point where sales were just slow enough that we could keep up with ordering the next round of inventory. We took the money we made from sales, and we bought another 500 units. Then, in the next round, we bought 1,000 units. We just kept rolling the money back in, over and over, as the company grew. It was pure bootstrapping. In retrospect, I wish we'd been even more aggressive at the beginning, but we feared what would happen if we placed that first huge order and the product didn't sell.

For a lot of people, the biggest hurdle is *not* placing that preliminary order, but rather finding the money to avoid running out of stock faster than it can be replaced.

Some entrepreneurs raise a lot of money, giving them the flexibility to make mistakes. If you're like Michael Dubin and you raise $100,000 from a group of investors (or, heck, from your rich uncle), then my hat goes off to you. Having money allows you to make mistakes, lose money, and optimize over time. It also allows you to optimize for sales instead of profits. Most entrepreneurs don't have that luxury, so they are always walking a fine line between funding the growth and optimizing their personal profits.

That's why, at the beginning, you might have to use price as a way to control the speed of sales. If your product is selling too fast, you might have to scramble to fund your next order. If cash flow becomes a problem, then it's an indicator your price point may be too low. You may need to increase your price until sales move at a manageable level, allowing you to easily restock your product before it sells out.

I get a lot of pushback against raising prices. "But my competitor sells for less than me *already!*" people say. But you are not your competitor. If you are doing the exact same thing as your competitor, then you deserve to go out of business. Focus on your *customer*, not your competitor. One of my mentors, Kevin Nations, has his own rule of pricing that I like: Find out what the customer wants, find out what solving their problem is worth to them, then charge them a *little bit less* than that.

More sales are not necessarily better, especially if that means dropping your price. Most people think higher-volume sales are the goal, but that's not always the case. Kia sells more cars than Cadillac, but the profit margins are higher on the latter. I've seen a lot of people play the volume game and end up getting caught dropping their prices to the point where they can barely turn a profit. That quickly results in a race to the bottom. I would much rather have moderate sales with a high profit margin and a raving fan base over high sales that can't scale. A high-margin product makes it much easier to scale because you have more money to spend on advertising or rolling out second products.

One of my friends, Drew Canole, started a juice company called Organifi. There were already a ton of juice powders on the market, but Drew went with a premium pricing strategy—instead of selling for $19 to $29 as his competitors, he charged $70 for his thirty-day supply. That gave him the flexibility to create an amazing product, and it gave him the profit margin to advertise it to new customers.

Organifi charges two or three times as much as its competitors and outsells most of them. If it had worried about competitors, it would be struggling to sell a $29 product and wondering why it couldn't generate sales, even though its product is better than its competitors. I see that happen all the time.

Here's a quick marketing tip: If you listen to podcasts, you've definitely heard an ad at some point for one of the following: Casper Mattress, Blue Apron, Harry's Razors, Stitch Fix, or Brooklinen. The list goes on and on. When Drew was first scaling Organifi, I recommended he advertise on other people's podcasts. It gave the brand a huge surge of momentum. Podcast ads can be outrageously effective, but it's nearly impossible to afford that type of advertising if you're selling a low-margin product. If you are going to pay for endorsements, influencers, or any form of advertising, you need the profit margin to be able to scale. There's just no way to afford that kind of exposure if you're selling a $29 product.

Hammer Down the "Who" Behind Your Product

One of our Sheer Strength products was, at one point, the second most popular on the market. This should have felt like a huge accomplishment, but the win was dulled by the fact that no matter what we did, we just *could not* beat out our number-one competitor.

I could have shouted from the rooftops that our product was better and half the price. I could have blogged about studies that proved our product had a superior ingredient profile, sourcing, and research.

It wouldn't have mattered; this competitor outsold us two to one, and got better reviews to boot.

Why was this product outselling us two to one, while being twice the price and *lower* quality?

The difference was *who*: They were only targeting an older demographic with disposable income. We were targeting young guys, like us. They were targeting the segment of the market that was willing to spend more money because they were addressing a specific pain point. Our competitor's product was specifically branded for their demographic, and they crushed us. The hungriest segment of the market ignored us—we didn't look like we were "for them."

People will always pay a premium to solve *their* specific problem. That's why we choose brands—because they are *for us*. This is why you absolutely *must* hammer down the "who" behind your product. If you can speak directly to your

Roxelle is one of my favorite case studies because she focused so much on her *person* that she could sell *anything* and still be successful. If her swimsuits stop selling, she could sell a number of other products and still have a million-dollar business. Entrepreneurs get so caught up in the product that they forget about the *people* behind it. Roxelle did the opposite, and she can sell whatever she wants. I had Roxelle on my podcast to ask her about her story. You can listen to it at Capitalism.com/best.

target market, you can charge twice the price while creating loyal fans. If you're just trying to sell as many products to as many people as possible, then you really can only compete on price.

If you're attempting to bootstrap your business, it's even more important to dial in your customer base. You will need that profit margin to roll into additional products. If you don't know who you're trying to target, it'll be impossible to charge the premium prices you need to build that revenue.

One of my students, Roxelle Cho, is a great example of an entrepreneur who has been rewarded for knowing her customer extremely well. When she built her swimwear company, Fused Hawaii, she set out to inspire women to be more comfortable in their bodies. To do this, she came up with a very simple product: a one-piece swimsuit that's both comfortable and universally flattering. She started talking about women's issues on Facebook Live, and she built a raving fan base. When it came time for her to launch her product, she pre-sold her inventory before it was even in stock. When she pre-sold through the first batch, she raised her price—but the orders kept coming in. She kept raising the price, but people kept buying—even though they knew that the suits wouldn't be ready for weeks! She couldn't keep her bathing suit in stock, but the money kept coming in to fund more orders. That's a fun way to fund a business! Roxelle started with a great product, but the real secret to her success was that she knew her customer extremely well.

You Need $10,000

In the Capitalism Conference's very first year, we had three keynote speakers: Gary Vaynerchuk (he's a wonderful person), Grant Cardone (meh), and Robert Herjavec from *Shark Tank*.

While onstage with Robert, I asked him what the number-one thing people from *Shark Tank* invest the money they receive from a deal in. He said, "Money for inventory." That surprised me, so I asked him to clarify. "When it's time to go, you got to go, baby," he said.

When you've got a winning product, you can't lose momentum by running out of stock. After you've bootstrapped your product and started taking sales, your focus must immediately turn to keeping stock— sometimes that means securing money to keep enough inventory to keep building the snowball.

I recommend having at least $5,000 to $10,000 ready to deploy the moment you need it. You need this money to bridge the gap that's inevitably going to happen once your product starts quickly selling out. It doesn't mean you'll have to use it, but you'll be ready if you do. If you don't have $10,000 rolling around, then you need to go out and get *access* to $10,000.

Some first-time entrepreneurs panic when they hear this, but your $10,000 doesn't have to come out of your own pocket. Your job as an entrepreneur is to get access to resources. My mentor, Travis, calls it "thinking like a producer." Movie producers don't finance films with their own bank accounts. They also don't write the script or do the acting.

Instead, they find the right script, hire the right actors to sell tickets, and then they raise the money to fund the film.

An entrepreneur does the same thing. You have the ideas. You're not physically making the product; you have a manufacturer do that. It's your job to make the connections and manage the money. There are several ways to get the capital you need. Only one of those ways is to take it from your own bank account.

Your own resources aren't your only resources, either. The money could come from a line of credit, a loan taken out against your house, or an option with an investor. It could be money from Kickstarter or Kabbage.com or Amazon Lending. The money could come from anywhere, really—it's just up to you to go find it.

Here's an inventory tip: One benefit to placing a huge order is you have some wiggle room to negotiate with your suppliers. When you're only ordering 100 units at a time, you're going to pay the retail rate. But the more you order, the more negotiating power you have. Sometimes, a bigger order knocks down your per-unit price by up to 30 to 50 percent. It's a huge boon to the long-term growth of your business to be able to make a large order that drives down the COGS (cost of goods sold).

If You Decide to Raise Capital

The fastest way to raise capital is to bring on an outside investor. If that investor is willing to be an advisor or a strategic contact, it can be a huge benefit to your growth. And contrary to popular belief, outside investors are usually open to investing in new ideas.

Yet nearly every day, I see well intentioned entrepreneurs botch their pitches to potential investors. You just tell them about your business and ask for $10k for inventory, right? No. It's important to remember that investors aren't interested in your ideas but their return on investment. There has to be a clear plan for success in order for that money to go to work.

As a potential investor, I'm looking at your business plan. Specifically, I want to know how that money will be spent to make the business grow faster. Most importantly, who is your potential audience, and where are they? How are you getting in front of them? What are your plans for follow-up products? How are you allocating the money, and how are you planning to reach potential customers?

A lot of people are just looking for a Band-Aid. They'll approach an investor with the following pitch: "I'm out of cash. I need an infusion or I'm out of business. Can you solve my problem?"

No investor ever said, *Shut up and take my money!*

Raising money on an idea is really hard (and stupid). Raising money to fix a problem is even harder. Raising money to amplify what's already working? That's a slam dunk.

From an investor standpoint, I want to see how my money is going to grow the brand. The purpose of money is to make things go *faster*. It's great that you've got a strong product that's selling well, but do you have two or three other product ideas you can roll out to the same customer? Because ten grand might help you bridge this one gap, but it's not going to provide a return if you don't have a solid idea for your brand and more ideas that you can sell.

Remember that in the long run, a product does not create a million-dollar business, but a *brand* does. Ask yourself the question, *Is this investment going to grow a company, or are we looking to just patch a fulfillment problem?* The former excites me, and the latter just makes me feel used.

For example, someone approached me at one of my conferences and pitched me on investing in a feminine hygiene product. As little as I know about feminine hygiene, it did solve a major pain point. And the total market potential was in the hundreds of millions.

So I looked at him and said, "Okay, so what has stopped you from rolling this out?"

"I don't have money to get it started," he said.

I passed.

No one wants to fund an idea with no momentum. If you aren't willing to do the work to even develop a prototype, then you haven't shown any initiative that money is going to be well spent. I once heard it said that "money is attracted to movement." Show movement, and the money will follow. Your investors want to see that their money is going to be put to wise use. That means showing them what products you're going to roll out, how the money will be used to acquire new customers, and what momentum is already being built.

And, to be totally transparent, the opportunity at your fingertips if you do this right is *huge*.

There is always more money than there are good ideas. Investors will literally buy up crappy companies because there aren't enough good (let alone great) companies for sale. At the same time, there are an abundance of businesses that were never able to cross certain monetary hurdles and so are sitting on the market endlessly, never getting sold. Most buyers will not look at a business priced under a million dollars, and they won't look at a business that doesn't have revenue of at least a million dollars, which is why the *12 Months to $1 Million* process is so important.

Pro tip: When pitching to an investor, do not ask them for money. Ask for advice. Tell the investor you've been pursuing an opportunity, and explain the momentum that you have. Tell them that you've run into funding challenges. Tell them that you want to place larger inventory orders to serve your growing audience. Then tell them how much money you think you need. Finally, ask them, "How would you fund the growth of this business if you were me?"

Asking for money puts people on the defensive. Asking for advice opens them up. Watch how fast money shows up.

Crowdfunding

If you don't want to take on an investor, crowdfunding with a site like Kickstarter is another option.

I have a student, Sophie, who wanted to start a business aligned with her mission to reduce waste in the world. She created a reusable lunch box and started off selling it on Amazon. It was a modest success, but being able to place big enough orders to keep inventory in stock was putting a huge strain on her cash flow. She needed capital to scale up production.

It wasn't that Sophie couldn't have found investors—I, for one, would have been happy to invest in her company. But when she weighed the cost of taking money from an investor and giving up a chunk of her company versus keeping control, she decided to raise money via Kickstarter instead.

The benefit of crowdfunding on Kickstarter goes beyond raising money. You're effectively creating exposure and superfans—a horde of customers who are literally *invested* in the success of your business. Furthermore, you're not just getting money; you're recruiting customers as well.

Here are a few must-haves for running a successful Kickstarter campaign that puts you on the map and gets you the capital you need:

1. You need a great video. The most important element is that the video communicates a specific *emotion*. Sophie's video was recorded on her iPhone, but it was purpose-driven and rooted in emotion. At the very least, you need a video that explains what you're doing, why, and where you're going next.

Note that you don't need professional equipment to put a good video together. Plenty of people create compelling videos using only their smartphones. There are tons of tutorials out there on how to do this. Educate yourself on YouTube.

2. You need a list of at least ten ideal customers in your network (friends, co-workers, etc.) who are excited about what you're doing. Ask them to share your Kickstarter with their networks, which means their friends, their church groups, their fans, and especially their social media followers. This will be just enough exposure to get the ball rolling.

Sophie didn't have a huge audience; she simply shared her video on her personal Facebook page and asked her friends to do the same. That was enough to get things moving.

3. You need at least one micro-influencer who can help spread the video's message. It's time to go out and knock on doors to find that influencer. These could be Facebook groups, Instagrammers, bloggers, YouTubers, or podcasters. The only requirement is that this influencer has at least 10,000 eyeballs on their page or account. Ten thousand really is the magic number. At that level, the influencer isn't so big that they will ignore you, but they are big enough that their influence helps spread the word.

Sophie didn't know any influencers, so she contacted the leader of an eco-friendly Facebook group that had 20,000 members. She asked if she could talk about her Kickstarter in the group, and they agreed. That community ravenously shared and supported Sophie's Kickstarter campaign.

Just like any business, people want to know what's different about what you're offering. As with any marketing venture, it's your job to work like hell to get your information in front of the right people. Make a hit list of people you need to connect with to raise awareness about this launch.

Sophie ended up raising more than $25,000 in pre-orders for the product. She was expecting more like $5,000, so she really had to hustle to fulfill those orders! Luckily, with Kickstarter you have a bit more time for fulfillment than you do on Amazon, so she was able to deliver.

One of the most helpful trainings for using Kickstarter is available for free on Tim Ferriss's blog. Tim documents a campaign, along with examples and specific wording to smash all goals, on this post: www.tim.blog /kickstarter.

She used that capital and that momentum to roll out product after product, and she used the exposure from the Kickstarter campaign to get more press in her local area and online. A few years later, Sophie's business was nearing $10 million in sales. Not bad for an idea that started with a $5,000 goal!

Good Debt and Bad Debt

If you don't like the idea of giving up a piece of your company and crowdfunding sounds too labor intensive, taking out a loan to get you over the bridge is your other option. People are generally averse to the idea of taking out loans, but you can't consider debt in a vacuum. There's good debt and bad debt. The way you calculate if debt is good or bad is how it's used. Good debt produces return on investment (ROI), and bad debt is merely money spent.

Borrowing money to buy a fancy car is a bad use of debt. The car loses value as soon as you drive it off the lot, so the ROI is negative. Your money is no longer working for you; it's just gone. But, if you're using debt to buy something with a higher rate of return, that's *good* debt. That debt will ultimately make you money. For example, if you take out a loan to buy a house, and you rent the house out at a profit, then that's a good-use debt.

Bank loans are your best bet for affordable debt, and the Small Business Administration is one of the best sources of low-cost debt in the world. Its drawback? Time. Getting approved can take months.

One potential source of good debt is Kabbage.com, which offers crowdfunded loans for businesses. It's best used carefully, however, because it has really high interest rates—often, somewhere between 20 to 30 percent. Why would you use a service that's so expensive? *Because it's still less expensive than running out of inventory.*

If you're going to borrow money at 20 percent because you're going to use that money to buy inventory at $10 and sell it for $50, then you've now traded a 20 percent interest rate for a 500 percent return. Most of the time that's a pretty good trade.

I use strategic debt in my business when I can reliably predict my ROI. If I know I'm going to sell my inventory and get a 200 percent ROI on that purchase, then it makes sense to pay 10 percent or more on a loan. That frees up a lot of cash to use in other areas of business.

If you sell on Amazon or use Shopify for your online store, these services often release funding options for businesses with at least six to twelve months of sales history. Amazon's program is (predictably) called Amazon Lending, and it's one of the best sources of debt because it's affordable and fast. However, you must be consistently selling on Amazon before this option becomes available to you.

One Caveat to Debt

While there is nothing inherently wrong with debt, I would caution anyone against using debt at the very beginning of an idea—taking out loans for an unproven concept is a fast route to financial disaster.

Daymond John, the CEO of FUBU and a regular investor on *Shark Tank,* spoke onstage at the Capitalism Conference. He explained how debt can cripple a business. If you take out $100,000 for a business, it's easy to get distracted by storefronts and packaging, without ever taking sales. Wait until you have predictable sales to take out debt.

One of my most famous YouTube videos is about how to use debt to create passive income. It's a video about leveraging what I call ROI arbitrage. It's borrowing against your house, for example, to buy a website that's producing 25 percent per year in passive income. Borrowing 5 percent to make 25 percent is a good leveraging of debt.

Borrowing money to spend it or borrowing money to make speculative investments is *bad* debt. For example, buying into cryptocurrency is a kind of speculation. People would say they were "investing" in cryptocurrencies. No, they were speculating on the price going up and down. That's gambling.

When you have a product that's not yet proven to be marketable to customers, you're speculating. You're guessing. This is a bad time to borrow against your home or take out a business loan. I don't recommend going into debt to start a new business. Use debt to sustain and *grow* your business, knowing that the payments will come out of *future sales.*

One of my students and business associates has an investment banking background, and he saw the challenge that new entrepreneurs have when funding their inventory. He rounded up some of his investment banking buddies and started a company designed to get entrepreneurs the capital that they need to get past the "inventory hump." They specialize in getting sellers affordable capital *fast,* without causing stress for the entrepreneur. I love it when an entrepreneur sees a problem and creates a win-win solution—that's capitalism in action! You can find funding options like this at Capitalism.com /funding.

Once you have predictable sales, then you know there's an ROI to your business. Now you can *invest* more into it. That's when it's a good idea to raise money, go all in, or borrow to be able to scale the business. But not until that point. There's a chasm of difference between the two.

Another thing to note is that debt should always go into scaling inventory, not advertising or other costs. Debt has to be paid back, so use it on *predictable* expenses. You're not guaranteed an ROI on advertising; but if your inventory is guaranteed to sell, then you can be confident that you'll be able to settle up the debt it took to buy that inventory.

How to Know If You Need Money

Money is an amplifier, not a magic wand. If you have a bad idea, money just amplifies that bad idea. If it's a good idea, it can spread that idea to new customers. So how do you know the difference?

My first question for you: Have you proven that you can predictably turn $10,000 into at least $20,000? Show me the sales numbers from rolling out your first round of inventory. Money needs to have a strategic reason, and it needs to provide an ROI. How will the use of that money result in a more profitable, more successful business?

My second question: How are you taking your sales? If you have a built-in audience (from an influencer or a social media following), you might be able to pre-sell all $10,000 worth of product via Kickstarter or as a private sale. Take pre-orders and use that money to purchase your stock, and then pass the bill directly to your customers.

If you're having trouble keeping up with demand, or if you want to go bigger and have a reasonable plan to invest more money, then you can present your opportunity to an investor. While you're shopping for a good investor, you can fund the business with small microloans from companies such as Kabbage.com and UpFund.

If you don't know what route to go, don't go into debt. Raise your price. Focus on *higher profits* rather than acquiring funding. When in doubt, *wait*. Make a list of investors who you might want to work with, and tell them what you're up to. Then, take the time to allow the opportunity to present itself. Maybe you meet an influencer along the way, and you know that it will cause inventory constraints. Perhaps you get picked up by a major news outlet, and it puts a strain on inventory. That's when you make the call to your investor list.

Above all, focus on sales and proving your product. Most people are waiting for money so they can make a move. In reality, they have it backward: Money *follows* movement.

Funding your business isn't a matter of getting the money to push your product but a matter of creating enough momentum to attract the money you need. However, if you follow the steps in the next chapters, that momentum will snowball *very* quickly.

Entrepreneur Spotlight: AJ Patel

Back in 2013, AJ was looking for a new opportunity. For ten years he'd tried his hand at an array of businesses, with ups and downs, some success, and a lot of failures. In high school he had a web hosting business that made $5,000 a month. Then in college, he made six figures doing internet marketing. But both those businesses fell away. By 2013, he was ready for something new. He wanted to try his hand at selling a physical product.

AJ looked for something based in the United States that he could really get behind. Having had issues with his skin ever since he was young, he started a line of skincare products. There was a lot of demand, and he could relate to the customer.

He started by learning how to make sales on Amazon with Argan oil—a natural skin and hair care product.

Two weeks after launch, he was making $1,000 a day.

He knew this was it. People were actually buying what he was selling. He decided to add fuel to the fire: He started a second product and went all in with $40,000 of credit card and personal loan debt to bolster the business.

I said earlier that I'm debt-averse, but this is an example of a time when debt worked very, very well for an entrepreneur. AJ's gamble paid out big: After about three months, he was making more than $100,000 a month and was on track for a million-dollar year. And just thirteen months after his first Argan oil sale, he'd blown far beyond that million-dollar-a-year mark. He was making seven figures every single month.

AJ's path wasn't without its stumbles. In that first year, he tried to do *everything* in the business, which was a real learning experience. He finally realized going it alone just wasn't scalable. He needed help. He began hiring, discovering that to be successful you need a really good team that's collectively smarter than you alone. "Basically," he told me, "you need a team that will mask your weaknesses."

As the business grew, he built his team faster, became quicker at delegating work, and learned to be a better leader. He focused on scalable infrastructure, thinking about the resources he'd need in six months or a year, so he could get ahead in hiring the right people.

After a couple of years, AJ had close to twenty products in his brand. Every new item built on what he knew his consumers wanted: a wider selection of natural skincare products. He added deodorants, moisturizers, and toners, and paid attention to see how the market reacted.

As his business matured, so did his process of adding new products. Instead of guessing what his consumers wanted and then measuring sales, he proactively aligned his product selection with his brand values. He looked closely at his product portfolio and tweaked it, cleaning up the product ingredient list, making everything really natural, and refreshing the branding.

"These days, anything you build *has to have* a strong brand component," he said. "I don't think that was necessarily true when I started back in 2013. These days, you have to go beyond just a product-based business. You have to focus on your *why*."

With the success of his brand and the support of his team, AJ was able to start four more businesses in as many years. One was TriNova, a brand selling home, auto, and boat products, which he sold at the end of 2016 for a very impressive dollar amount.

But even before he sold TriNova, he launched a pet supplements brand, and then added health and wellness supplements to his portfolio. These brands were successful enough to get interest from a private equity firm. He divested a portion to private equity while keeping a good chunk of ownership and staying on the board of directors, so he can help however possible.

Most recently, he launched a brand called Smooth Viking, which sells men's beard and hair care products. He also started his own private equity company to invest in other businesses. All this started by selling his first product on Amazon.

"People are always afraid of failing, but failures can provide really valuable insights and lessons, which give you more confidence," AJ said. "Most people don't take action because they're afraid of losing money or of what someone might say about them. But when you take action, you'll at least learn something, even if you don't make money."

Every year, AJ learns more than he did the year before. More than anything, he's learned that success really comes down to people. People help you scale businesses, and that's what allowed him to run five different brands at the same time, and to ensure those brands align with his reason for being.

6

Step Four:
Stack the Deck

I was twenty-one when I started following famous entrepreneur Gary Vaynerchuk. I had just graduated from college, and I was in that self-discovery period, trying really hard to find direction. My lifelong dream was to own the Cleveland Indians, but I had no idea how I was going to get there. Around that time, I saw some dude announce at a conference that he intended to own the New York Jets.

I snapped to attention. *This guy is ten years older than me, and ten years closer to the same goal I have,* I thought. *I'm going to just watch what he does. Maybe he can shed some light on the path.*

I've watched Gary closely ever since, and he was one of the first guests I booked at the very first Capitalism Conference. I wanted to discover what his plan was to own a major sports franchise. What I discovered is that his entire focus is on building the engine that allows him to create and acquire brands that can be worth billions of dollars.

When it comes to stacking the deck in your favor, there's no one better than Gary. He spent years delivering content and building an audience that follows and trusts him. That content gives him leverage, exposure, and, most importantly, relationships. Put simply, he has resources at his fingertips he can tap into to help build or scale any brand he touches.

What fascinates me most about Gary's strategy is that he can use his audience to launch brands. In fact, he's used that leverage to launch a speaking bureau, a sports agency, and several consulting agencies. When he launched his winery, Empathy Wines, I was among the first in line to place a big order. I also flew to New York City to interview Gary about the launch, where he reframed the strategy for me: "I have no expectation of converting any of the audience that I already have into customers of any product that I sell," he said. "Think about it—I give away most content for free. The amount of sales I've made in return doesn't even come close to balancing the amount of content I give away.

"I put out content for the sake of putting out content. I'm comfortable asking my audience to consider my product if they're already in the market for sneakers or wine, but I have no expectation of conversion. That's not why I'm putting out content. In fact, the hucksters I make fun of, who are selling tons of products to their audience from moment one—they're actually *killing me* in the short term. Their sales crush mine.

"I'm not in this for the short term. I want my audience to show up at my fucking *funeral.* And I *mean that.* I don't need my audience's money. I'm going to sell way more bottles of Empathy Wine to people who have never heard of me. But building VaynerMedia is the way I'm setting up the play for Empathy, and for the brands I buy in the future."

I realized that Gary was playing this *very* differently from everyone else out there. "You want to be happy? Give without the expectation of receiving," he said. "You want to be *really unhappy*? Give only for the expectation of people giving you something in return. Humans don't act that way. That won't happen."

It's true that Gary expects little of his audience—after all, his following isn't just a following of wine lovers—but that audience *still* has the power to command tens of thousands of wine bottle sales. Furthermore, the relationships he's built have opened up the door for that brand. In a podcast interview with me, Empathy Wines CEO Jonathan Troutman told me that its strategy wasn't to depend on Gary's audience, but that it certainly lit the first spark, instead of starting at dead zero.

The wine, of course, still has to be good, and the brand needs to stand on its own, but his audience serves as the initial "spark" to get the product moving off the shelves. In the same way that Tim Ferriss can put a brand on the map by talking about it on his podcast, Gary can do it with his own audience—even if the product isn't perfectly tailored to his entire audience. That's the power of having even a little bit of attention.

Alcohol brands have sold for billions of dollars (George Clooney's tequila brand, Casamigos, was sold for a cool billion dollars just four years post-launch), so that "spark" could become the flame that buys Gary the New York Jets.

You don't have to build an audience the size of Gary's to completely alter the course of your business. If you do just a fraction of what we outline next, you'll set yourself up to quickly put your company on the map, sprint toward twenty-five sales per day (and eventually 100 sales per day), and clear the million before your first year is done.

Similar to Gary, I post all my best content for free on my podcast. You can hear my conversations with him, as well as the interview with the CEO of Empathy Wines, at Capitalism.com/best.

Welcome to the Grind

If we wanted to make earning money really simple, we could boil it down to two steps: pick something to sell and sell it. Most people never make it through the first step of deciding what to sell. Instead, they sell their time in the form of a 9-to-5 job.

Deciding what your business is going to sell, who your customers are going to be, and getting your product made is no small task. That's why most people never even make it to this point. When you make these decisions, you are nearly halfway home. However, as the old adage goes, nothing really *happens* until *something is sold*.

Everything up to this point is simply getting into the game. You have a product to sell. Now, it's time to play the game. Right now, you don't know how to play the game, so the first few months of the game are a grind.

During this time, you will likely obsess over every detail, and you will overthink every decision. When the chaos starts to get to you, take peace in the fact that your goal is incredibly simple. Your only job during this period is to *take a sale*. That's it. You will feel tempted to make it complicated, to follow a slew of different people's advice, or to create complex sales systems. You will want to get distracted by reading marketing blogs and chasing every opportunity that falls into your lap.

But you have just that one job: take a sale.

Whenever I feel stressed, I remind myself that my job in business is to take a sale. If I'm having a bad day, I'll often make a list of prospective customers, or put something on social media that talks about one of my products. Then, I call those customers personally, email them, or send them a message. My goal is to take one sale. It's hard to express how much that can turn my day around.

Sometimes, you have to think very small in order to focus, but doing that creates momentum that very quickly builds. Right now your focus is 100 percent on taking sales, and you will have to resist "big thinking" to do the work necessary to take those orders.

Thankfully, I have coached hundreds of entrepreneurs through this process, and believe me, it used to be *much* harder. It used to be that entrepreneurs would spend three to four months just getting their finished products in front of enough people to take a sale. Today we know better. Today we know that we can complete "The Grind" in thirty days or less.

We do that by "stacking the deck."

How to Guarantee Sales from Day One

You don't need to be a social media celebrity, or even have a following, to guarantee sales of your product on the first day. You just need enough eyeballs to put the cards in your favor.

That's what led me to utter these three words: *"I love yoga."*

By no means am I the first person—or even the millionth person—in recent history to say those three words on social media. The impact they had on my business, though, was incalculable. Those three words were essentially enough to get me in front of as many people as I needed to launch a successful and profitable brand.

Back in 2013, I was working with many new entrepreneurs who were excited about the opportunity to start a business. However, they sometimes got frustrated when it came time to take sales for their product. They did a ton of research to find their first product. They did the hard work of getting samples and working with suppliers. Then, they set up their Amazon store and . . . crickets.

I call that "the hump." It's when you do a lot of work to get your product ready for sale, and then you hit a barrier to the next steps. And it's why the first few months in business are called The Grind.

If new business owners don't get sales *right away*, they often get discouraged, anxious, and worried. Sometimes, they think about quitting before they even have a chance to get started. But if they make it over this "hump," they sail toward success. Fast sales out of the gate, on the other hand, gives them the momentum to keep going and keep growing.

That's why so many of my students are so profitable and successful. In The Grind we work almost exclusively on getting sales as fast as possible.

While I was coaching some of them through the process, I heard one of my peers utter, "Man, I'm so jealous of established companies who already have customer lists. They can just market their product to people who have already bought in the past. I mean, look at Apple—they have people waiting in line to get the next product! Wouldn't it be nice if you could launch a product to a group of people ready to buy your product *the day you had it ready?*"

Until that point, I'd been teaching sales and marketing strategies to help my group of new entrepreneurs get through the hump. Those strategies worked, but they took time and effort to really kick in.

When I heard my friend utter those words, I wondered, *Is there a way for me to "stack the deck" so that sales come rushing in on the very first day?* Maybe we didn't have the customer list or the budget that big companies have, but still, I wondered if I could get people lining up, ready to buy the product the day it was ready.

At the time, Sean and I were launching our yoga business, and I was documenting the whole thing for my students. I called him one Saturday morning and asked for an update on the state of yoga mats we had ordered. "They are on a boat, on their way from the supplier that we chose on Alibaba," he said. "They won't be at Amazon for like eight weeks."

He was frustrated. We had done all this work, and now we had to wait *eight weeks* for the product to get here?

However, I saw that as an opportunity. I told Sean, "Okay, buddy, that means we have eight weeks to 'stack the deck' in our favor. Our job now is to do everything we can to ensure that we have people ready to buy the very first day that our yoga mats are ready for sale."

"How the heck do we do that?" Sean asked.

We started talking about our options. Should we blog about yoga and build traffic to our website? What if we made videos and launched the product on YouTube? We could build an email list, or we could partner with a big yoga community.

All those ideas sounded great, but they would take longer than eight weeks to kick in. Instead, we looked for the quickest, simplest, and fastest way to get people to line up ready to buy our yoga mats.

At the time, Facebook had just released Business Pages, and it was getting a lot of free traffic. We created a small Facebook page around the topic of yoga, and we called it *I Love Yoga*. Straightforward enough, right? The audience data collected was broad, but that didn't matter; I knew that anyone who liked that page was into yoga, and anyone who was into yoga would buy yoga mats. I'd already identified the products people who are into yoga buy as well. All I needed from there was enough of an audience to be able to talk up the yoga products I was planning to sell.

We started sharing content on the page to get our followers to like and share that content. We spent $10 per day on advertising to build the following. And we engaged with our followers in the comments. After about thirty days, we had around 3,000 people who liked our page.

But we did one more thing that was the *most important piece of it all*: We documented our product release on the *I Love Yoga* Facebook page. We didn't brag about the product or try to sell it; we simply talked about our product by showing the prototype process, explaining the difference in our product, and sharing every change we made to it based on feedback from people like them. We showed them that we'd added a thicker strap to our yoga mat simply because that was what they said they wanted. We showed them that we listened to them, that we wanted to hear what they had to say, and that we wanted to serve their needs.

As we were building that Facebook page, Sean and I knew that as soon as we were ready to launch we'd have an audience who was ready to buy. Or, for all you poker players out there, we had stacked the deck in our favor.

Getting over the Hump

The goal is to get enough eyeballs in one place to get a spark lit. It's a bit like using a magnifying glass to start a fire. Can you point *just enough* power at your target to get it to ignite?

Using Facebook to build up a hungry audience will work for as long as Facebook continues to exist, but the tactics you use may change with the times. And since the internet is always evolving, new opportunities are always opening up. However, the principles are timeless. Your job is to "stack the deck" so that you have people waiting to buy your product the day it comes out. You will do this by running advertising to a central place where you can contact your audience, engage that audience with content that appeals to them, and document the launch of your product, so that they're primed and ready to buy when it's ready.

Getting to this point is hard work: deciding who your audience is, developing your product, figuring out how to bring your product to market, and placing your order for inventory. Add to that the fact that you've spent anywhere between $500 and $5,000 on that inventory. Then suddenly you hit "the hump." The time between ordering your inventory and it being ready for sale, which can range anywhere from two weeks to three months, can feel like the longest wait of your life. Sure, it will be exciting to hear that your product is manufactured, shipped, put on a boat by a freight forwarder, and heading across the ocean, but the anticipation is like waiting for your first baby to arrive (ask me how I know!).

If you start on Kickstarter, you can pre-sell a lot of product, gaining faster sales momentum. If you're selling on Amazon, you can't go live with sales until there's actually inventory at the warehouse. Either way, stacking the deck with ready-to-buy customers will strike a match that brings a roaring fire to life. Not only does that give you the momentum and the energy to keep growing but it also helps you rank for keywords on both Kickstarter *and* Amazon. The buzz you generate also gets people talking about you on social media and sharing the product with their friends. It makes getting reviews easier, too.

In other words, it would be a *big* mistake to avoid "stacking the deck." I have seen many would-be entrepreneurs with good ideas simply give up because they didn't get momentum fast enough. Following these steps could have saved them.

I want to point out that I might be an expert at this *now*, but I was really just guessing through the beginning of all this. Yes, I have a background in digital marketing that helped me to navigate this unknown terrain, but I was still *guessing* at the strategy. I was able to beat all my competitors because most people are doing nearly nothing to stack the deck. They're so focused on the moment their product goes live that they're not even considering how to boost that moment ahead of time. So, even if you only do this process with 20 percent competence, you're still going to be miles ahead of the game.

Your only goal at the end of the eight weeks, on launch day, is to have enough of a following to be able to move the first few hundred units of your product. That way, you can get that snowball rolling and get to twenty-five sales a day.

There are a ton of options for you to find that following to do this online. Facebook groups are free and easy to build, as are LinkedIn groups, and they each can have very high engagement. Some people use Instagram pages or other social media accounts, which work well as long as you can stand out. Some people just use their own personal Facebook pages, which can also do the trick. The important thing is attracting a few hundred people who are responsive and passionate, like you are conversing with a community.

That community will follow your product journey and support you when it comes time to launch. That will be the spark that takes you to twenty-five sales per day and beyond.

How Much of an Audience Do I Need?

Theoretically, 100 people in the same room, ready to buy on launch day, would be enough to start the fire.

The size of the audience matters less than the *responsiveness* of your community. Buying cheap traffic to a Facebook page won't give you as much momentum as dedicated email subscribers or a close community of Instagram followers. The goal is not to have a lot of passive followers; your goal is to have people lining up at the doors on launch day, ready to buy.

Yes, you can include your friends in this list. You can include your co-workers, and you can include the pizza delivery guy who needs your product. Heck, I know some people who launched their products with a private email or text thread with just a few dozen people. It wasn't ideal, but it worked. Remember, your goal is to get *just enough* people ready to buy on launch day that you kick-start the momentum.

I have found this formula to be helpful during this process:

1,000 followers + 10 personal contacts + 1 influencer = 100 sales

In other words, if you can get your brand in front of 1,000 people on your own using ads or content creation, then you have enough of a "public following" to smash launch day. On top of that, if you ask ten personal friends to join the launch, and you secure one micro-influencer, you will have the numbers you need.

When Sean and I had more than 1,000 followers on our Facebook page, we knew that we had enough of a fan base to begin the launch process. On top of that, we called our list of personal friends who did yoga. We knew that if one of our friends was into yoga, then he or she knew *other* people who also were. We told them what we were up to, gave them a free yoga mat, and asked if they would be willing to post about it on social media on launch day.

If you want to *really* knock it out of the park, add one micro-influencer to the mix to stoke the fire. In our case, that meant forming a partnership with one similar yoga page with at least 10,000 followers. That was 1,000 followers on our page, ten personal friends, and one micro-influencer. We knew that would be enough to get 100 sales on launch day. And if we were wrong, well, it was better than nothing!

You don't have to have everything perfect, but the more eyeballs, the better. If you only have 500 followers (or no following at all), but you still have personal friends and an influencer, *launch*. Go as hard as you can with the resources that you have.

Remember, most people get stuck here. They put their product up for sale and then they wait. They expect the internet gods to rain favor upon them in the form of sales. Do not follow their lead. Use whatever you have, whether that be a YouTube channel, a friend with a blog, or your own personal Facebook page, to start the fire.

My student Sophie, who I've mentioned before, followed this process with amazing success, even though she didn't have a big following or a lot of connections. When she ran her successful Kickstarter campaign, she documented the process on her personal Facebook page. She had no ad budget—her entire marketing plan just consisted of lining up a few hundred people, a few personal contacts, and a Facebook group—and she's been stoking the fire ever since. She recently emailed me to tell me that she had made $1 million in *a month* selling her reusable lunchboxes and other products.

That's one hell of a fire!

How Should I Build My Audience?

Social media whims can change from minute to minute. One second, a new Facebook feature is hot; the next, it's Instagram, Snapchat, LinkedIn, or whatever the cool new thing is (and it seems like you have to be twenty-two or younger to stay ahead). All of them are centered on what gets attention and what gets engagement. For the purposes of promoting your product on launch day, you can ignore the latest social media buzz—you don't need to become an expert on any specific platform. You just need to choose a way to get in front of your ideal "person" in a way that gets their attention and encourages them to follow your journey. Your best bet is to discover where your audience *already lives* and combine it with how you are comfortable communicating with them.

One of my students, for example, has an organization company. His audience is mostly women who are obsessed with perfectly organized closets, drawers, and the like. His audience already hangs out on Pinterest, so he puts his attention there. *I*, on the other hand, have never used Pinterest and would have a really hard time building an audience there. Since I like to talk about business, and it's natural for me to talk into a microphone, podcasting is my preferred method for building an audience. I can't get feedback from a podcast, so I send my audience to an email list so that I can communicate with my followers.

The process in this book will work with any platform as long as you share content, run ads, and actively engage with your community. If you're building up a brand you're personally excited about, then creating content on a blog, a podcast, or a video channel is your best bet. It'll enable you to attract long-term followers. If you're not a subject-matter expert when it comes to your market, then you'll want to run ads and bring people to a central location—a Facebook group, Instagram account, or an email list—because you need those 1,000 followers to be within your control.

Some people consider hiring out content creation or hiring a marketing agency at this stage in the process—but that's going too deep, too soon. Remember, you only need 100 people or so who buy at first launch to start building the snowball.

What the heck do you put in front of your audience to get them excited to follow you? And, more importantly, excited to buy on launch day?

All you need to do is document the building of your business. That's it. Post pictures of your prototype. Share videos of how nervous you are. Post a picture of one of your friends holding the finished product. Write posts about why you decided to serve this market.

On top of that, entering the conversation your community is having goes *a long way*. For example, if a new golfer hits the scene, and you are selling golf gear, do a blog post, video, or podcast about the new golfer's chances. Is he the next Tiger Woods? Or is the hype overblown?

If your community is buzzing about something, give your take on it. This will engage your audience and attract new ones, and it breaks up the content that's exclusively about your product launch.

You might also simply answer commonly asked questions among your audience. Make a list of five to ten questions that your person asks when they

> Shortcut: If you can get your message in front of 10,000 people or more, then you can jump directly to communicating with them about your new product line. If you (or one of your partners) already have an audience, it can be the "hack" to shortcut this process. Partnering with influencers and making them an official part of the brand is my favorite shortcut to put a brand on the map. If you have an advertising budget, spend some of it on sponsoring a related podcast or YouTube channel that already has the audience.

start their journey, and then create a piece of content around them. The blend of product pieces, engagement with your community, and commonly asked questions will get your tiny audience to rally around you.

One of my students, Colin, runs a company called Wild Foods (@ wildfoodsco on Instagram). He does a great job of mixing product, commentary, and questions into his public following. He started at zero and went through this exact process, and he's now crossed seven figures, with his brand carried by retail chains all over the country.

Ultimately, a brand is really just trust, and you are earning people's trust at this stage in the process. When people start to engage, they will bring their friends with them. People trust the personal opinions of their friends; that's why word-of-mouth advertising is so incredibly valuable to a business. You can stack the deck with that trust early by putting out your own personal opinions to groups of people already looking to you to solve their problems.

During this process, you may also start to get the attention of other influencers. That is a very, very good thing. One caveat, though: Nobody likes a cold call, even when there's no money involved. Approaching an influencer and asking them to feature or share your content isn't going to build a relationship—it's only going to make that person feel like a transaction.

The trick is not to *ask*, as in, "Hey, can I be on your show?" The trick is to give: "Here's a piece of content I made that I think your audience would love. Is there anything that your audience is struggling with that I could write about or speak to, in order to serve them?"

If you do that, you'll find that influencers will happily invite you onto their platforms to better serve their audiences. If you're a guest on someone's podcast and your content is helpful, you make that podcaster look good *and* you earn more followers—it's a win-win.

It will be slow and frustrating at first, but you have to do it. Answer every comment, and respond to each message. Just like a new diet or other life change, it will be hard to see the progress at first, but over a few weeks, you will gain the momentum that you need to hit pay dirt.

Prepping for Go Time

Everything in the lead-up to Day One is designed to prep your audience to buy from you on launch day. For Sean and me, that meant that the closer we got to Day One, the more promotional we got.

Our messaging wasn't over-the-top or pushy, but it was direct. "We're really excited about this product line. But we have some bad news: We were only able to order 500 of these for the first round. If you want one, leave a comment below and we'll put you on our special launch list so that you're first in line, ahead of everybody else, when they go live on April 30."

We weren't shy about selling the product or sharing the inventory constraints, and people responded. It worked. We took fifty sales out of the gate and fifty more sales shortly after that. Those people left reviews and told their friends, and we were soon doing fifty sales *per day* on that first product, which was the equivalent of a six-figure business. We knew we had a winner. Don't miss the opportunity to line up those hot leads so they're ready to buy on launch day.

You might think that your business is too small or your niche is too specific for a launch strategy to be applicable to you.

Two of my students, Jenna and Travis Zigler, are eye doctors. They started out selling sunglasses, but they wanted to release more products that reflected their expertise. They had a list of products they wanted to launch, but there didn't seem to be enough volume to support the purchase of more inventory.

One of these products was a spray for dry eyes. There's just not a lot of volume out there for people looking for a spray to relieve dry eyes.

They told me they were going to put up a Facebook group for people with dry eye syndrome. Even *I* thought that the following, which was only a few hundred people, would be too small to launch multiple products. "Guys," I told them, "that's a really small market. Maybe you should go a bit broader, and just offer general advice for eye health."

Against my advice, they started a Facebook group where they answered frequently asked questions about dry eyes. At the end of each week, they did a Facebook Live with their community. All these dry-eye sufferers started inviting their friends who they knew suffered from dry eyes as well, tagging one another and asking more questions. The doctors only built up a community of a few hundred people, but they were incredibly responsive and quick to engage, and the community loved it.

I was wrong.

When they finally launched their dry eye spray product, it blew up. The community rallied to support it, buy it, and review it. That product had extremely high profit margins, and they didn't have to pay for advertising as the community helped spread the word. That one product completely changed their business. They were able to launch other products to that same audience, tripling and eventually quadrupling their revenue. They now had the ability to test different ideas quickly, without having to worry about competition, price wars, or people who had thousands of more reviews than they did. They could predictably roll out products, and they built a multimillion-dollar business.

Your Hot List

One of the things that helps guarantee your success is developing a "hot list" of buyers who raise their hands and commit to buying your product on launch day. The process for doing this is stupidly simple.

Here's how it works: As you publicly talk about your product, you will inevitably have certain people who get more excited than others. I like to reward them by putting them "first in line." The more people who are first in line to buy my product, the better chances of my product's success.

For example, as I get closer to launch day, I start to get more promotional. I might post something like, "As you know, our yoga mats go on sale April 2! And this early in the process, it's really important that we get feedback from people who have been following us. Sadly, we only have a few hundred of them available, so I am holding a handful of them for followers who are raring and ready to go. If you want me to reserve one for you for the first twenty-four hours on launch day, comment 'I Want One' and I will add you to our hot list."

When you start saying that there is a limited supply of a product, you start to build up a mini buying frenzy. People will sign up for your hot list even if they were "on the fence" before. This buying frenzy creates momentum and allows you to sell your product even harder.

For example, I might follow up with a post like: "Wow! Over fifty people commented on my last post and said that they wanted one of our yoga mats. I'm so honored—thank you! I will be holding a total of 100 yoga mats to ensure that first-responders get their mat the day that it's available. Sadly, that means that even fewer will be available to the general public, so if you want on the first-in-line list, please comment 'First in Line' and I will add you to the hot list."

I like to bring my hot list into a separate communication channel—usually an email list, Slack channel, or private Facebook group, so that they feel like an insider. I remind them that they are getting advanced notice of the product going live. And when the product is ready on launch day, that small group of people will rush the doors to buy my product!

How to Stack the Deck

Again, your one goal during this stage of the process is to build a big enough audience to earn your brand at least 100 customers when you launch. Here's how you get those first 100 customers:

1. Identify where your target market already hangs out. Sometimes they're already following certain Instagram pages, they're in specific Facebook groups, or they watch particular YouTube channels.

2. Create a series of content directly targeted to that person. You can also start building relationships with the people who run those groups you found in the first step.

3. Document the process of your product. What's different about it? Why did you make certain decisions? How far are you from launch?

4. Start announcing when the product is going to be available. Build up your following, your network, and your content by responding to every comment, replying to every message, and sharing your opinion on topics within the community—and then let your followers know when they'll be able to buy your product.

5. Reach out to your own personal contacts and start lining up that one influencer. Many people discount the power of their own personal network. If you're passionate about or involved in the market to which you're speaking, then you absolutely know ten people who are customers in that market. If you're launching a CrossFit brand, then you know ten people who also do CrossFit and are posting about it on Facebook. It doesn't matter if these people aren't at the level of "influencer." If you're only trying to get 100 people to buy in the first part of your launch, then you only need these ten people to influence ten other people. Today, the average person has a few hundred Instagram followers and at least 100 Facebook friends. Line up ten of them, and you're in front of thousands of people. That's more than enough to do damage.

6. Finally, build your hot list. Start moving people to the front of the line so they can be one of the first people to try your product.

Real-World Stacked Decks

Roxelle Cho is one of my favorite students. She started Fused Hawaii, a handmade swimwear brand that empowers women to live comfortably in the skin they're in. Not long ago, Roxelle was making products in her garage, but then she gained the loyalty and support of a growing customer base through Facebook Live, Instagram, and emails. She didn't consider herself a marketer; she just showed up for her audience, which caused Fused Hawaii to scale incredibly fast. She quickly passed $120,000 in sales per month with only social media.

"I sell swimwear, but I don't consider Fused Hawaii a swimwear company," she told me. "When I started out, I was making handbags, screen-printed shirts, hats, anything I could make out of my garage. I named the company Fused because I was fusing together all my artistic instincts. I didn't know what I was doing, but I knew the business was something that was going to continue to shift through the years.

"Growing our audience's brand allows me to experience these incredibly cool moments with our customers as we grow. When something great happens, our first instinct is to share it. That's what all of this is about: growing alongside people."

Roxelle's swimwear mission was to differentiate from all the other brands out there selling confidence, both real and false. "As women, even when you feel good in your own skin, you're always going to reach a moment where you have a lack of confidence," she said. "So for the ideal Fused Hawaii woman, it's not just about feeling confidence or saying we're confident. It's more about taking the leap when you don't know the results or the outcome. It's about going in the direction of your beliefs and intention. As I've gotten really clear on my messaging, it's become clearer that it's not just about confidence; we're speaking to the girl who is going to take a risk and jump toward her dreams even when it's scary, not knowing where she's going to land, but knowing she'll be strong enough to stand when she does."

That message has vaulted Roxelle above other brands speaking to women.

"In Hawaii, *land of swimwear*, we're in our swimwear all the time," she said. "It's the most vulnerable piece of clothing there is. In Hawaii, we're out in public in our swimwear—in lingerie, basically. To feel confident in your skin in *that* state is the win for me, and what I want to bring to my audience with our messaging."

Roxelle's swimwear success came at the same time as her message. The two threads are intertwined. "I knew it was the product along with the story that really sold the brand. I was hearing from women who told me that for the first time, they felt comfortable out on the beach with their kids, or going to a party in a swimsuit. I'm not a designer! I was just making swimwear for myself, and slapping my logo on it. But it was the story, alongside the products made for real women, which built our audience."

Today, Roxelle can sell whatever she wants at whatever quantity she desires. Her customers buy months in advance, and she literally cannot keep up with the demand.

That's a nice problem to have.

When you have an audience, you can take more strategic risks, too.

The Flexible Dieting Lifestyle is a company I advise that sells healthy versions of favorite cheat meals. One of the co-founders, Zach Rocheleau, built his audience by posting recipes on Instagram, and it was all he needed to launch physical products.

"We had built a brand around solving a problem everyone has—turning 'cheat meals' into everyday meals," Zach told me. "One of our biggest hits was a recipe for protein cookie butter. It had great nutritional value, tasted great, and met our audience's cravings. But one thing they kept telling us was that, basically, they didn't want to make it themselves. They wanted to be able to just buy it."

It was new territory for Zach as he'd never done a physical product before. "We decided to just figure it out," he said. "We developed the product, came up with 10,000 units, and launched it with zero ad spend. All we did was show the product to our audience—put in front of their eyes this thing they'd been asking for—and tell them, *hey, here it is, swipe up to purchase.* And they did. We went through 10,000 units in a single week."

Zach focused on storytelling and building an audience with an emotional connection to his company. That emotional connection is the key point. You want customers who aren't price-shopping but who buy your product because they feel connected to you.

When Should I Hit the "Go" Button?

As your inventory inches its way across the ocean and gets closer to its arrival at the Amazon warehouse, you'll be able to more accurately pinpoint Day One: launch day.

A word of advice: Give yourself a time buffer. If you think your product is going to be available on Friday, schedule your launch for the following Wednesday. Hyping up a launch date only to be unable to take sales on that day is a huge waste of customer attention and engagement.

You may want to consider creating some sort of incentive for people to buy within the first few days. This could be a bonus or some sort of discount, like a BOGO deal. In general, I don't like pricing discounts—it can be incredibly difficult to pivot out of being seen as a discount brand—but it's okay in a launch period with the understanding that you'll probably never discount the price of the product again, except in special situations. Just make sure to include a firm deadline on the discount and stick to it. Be protective of your inventory, especially when you're doing extras. My preference is to have a bonus or add-on to make your product an irresistibly sexy buy in its first few days.

Sometimes, honest scarcity is the best incentive to buy. If you only have 500 units available, and you have 500 people on your launch list—not to mention the 1,000 people who follow you on Instagram, and all their friends who might see and share your content, too—then there will be people who aren't going to get to make a purchase. This kind of scarcity only drives more interest. In the customer's mind, scarcity equals value.

During the final seven days before your launch, you should talk about the launch *every* day: emailing your list, posting about it on social media, leveraging any influencer relationships you've built. Burn it into everyone's brain: *This product goes LIVE at 11 A.M. next Wednesday!*

The minute 11 A.M. hits, watch the floodgates open.

Be sure to temper your expectations for those first few days. It's easy to get caught up in the excitement of launch and the engagement your audience is showing you, and then be disappointed when you don't immediately sell out (which, again, you *do not* want to do!).

As long as you get at least 25 to 100 sales in the first few days (and if you do what I outline in this book, it's very rare that that *won't* happen), you'll have enough momentum to start to scale the business further. Remember the formula to get to $1 million: three to five products, at an average price point of $30, each getting twenty-five sales per day, equals a million-dollar business.

Once you reach twenty-five sales, your job becomes following up with those customers to get reviews. We'll talk about that in a later chapter, as I don't want to teach you to sprint before you start to walk. Your only job right now is to take a sale, and the best way to do that is by stacking the deck.

Entrepreneur Spotlight: Marvin Lee

Marvin Lee was a registered nurse with a very high-paying job from which he was almost fired.

Management was moving everyone around, and Marvin soon realized his job was in jeopardy. He'd also lost his passion for the work. He got into nursing to help people, and those parts of the job were amazing—but there were so many standards and policies and people telling him what he should be doing that those parts of the job he loved were getting lost.

Marvin had always wanted financial freedom, too. He'd had a bit of a rough upbringing, which had motivated him to make something of himself. So he'd been saving his money, but he didn't really know what to do with it.

He talked to some friends who were doing well with online businesses, and he wondered if it was possible for him also. During his research, he stumbled across my videos.

When he discovered that it was indeed possible for him, he partnered up with his best friend to get started. They began looking for a product that would be profitable and that they had the budget to compete with (they didn't have a lot of money they were willing to invest).

They discovered a unique fitness tool they could adjust for the yoga niche. Shockingly, there were zero competitors with a similar product in the yoga space. It was perfect.

A friend of Marvin's was in touch with manufacturers in China, and he got them amazing deals with a manufacturer. Having done his research, Marvin worked with the factory to make modifications based on reviews. The end result was the same basic product being sold as a general recovery tool but tailored to the yoga audience, and improved over all the other versions.

It was a huge hit. People absolutely loved it.

However, Marvin knew I recommend having three to five products to create a brand. While Marvin had a popular product on his hands, he didn't have a brand. And he found creating one really, really tough.

He didn't know how to define "brand" or put a neat box around it. People would tell him "brand" was his logo or how a customer felt when they saw the product, but what did that mean in terms of actionable steps?

He read books on marketing that were full of random stuff he couldn't apply to his business.

He knew that for branding, *different* was better. But what did it even mean to be different? Should they have a different color? A higher price? They struggled to figure out how to be different, and how to tie that into a brand theme that would serve the customer. It was hard to create an aligned brand when they'd never targeted a specific person. They'd just focused on creating a better product, but hadn't considered *who* they were serving.

Then he heard me in one of my videos hammering home the importance of audience and messaging. *Why don't I just talk to my audience directly?* he thought.

Marvin didn't post much on Instagram, or even have a large following, but he started taking the time to send direct messages to customers, asking them what they thought of the product.

"That was a total game changer" Marvin told me. "Having real conversations with people who loved the product made us understand who they were, and what products they might want next."

Even though it was only a few hundred people, Marvin's audience responded loudly.

He and his partner used the feedback they received to adjust their marketing, which resulted in more sales. They moved from just having a product to thinking about the person who would benefit from it and what he or she would use that product for. They always made sure that they were serving a *person*.

By the time competitors found their market and tried to copy them, Marvin and his partner were too far ahead. At that point, customers kept choosing them, thanks to all the reviews from real people.

Marvin has had a ton of success with just two products, but he plans to add at least three more. Then he'll be in a position to possibly sell the brand.

"If I could give one piece of advice to someone looking to start a products business, it's to make sure you know what you're doing first," Marvin said. "A lot of people say to take action, but don't rush. You'll make mistakes. Expensive ones."

Marvin and his partner didn't just test everything to see what worked. They thought things out. They considered all scenarios. "You also have to love learning," he told me. "If you don't continue learning, someone is going to outlearn you and become more successful." And in this game, learning means listening to your customers.

In business, there will always be people who want to copy you, which means each business is a dying business. If you're not forever evolving, you have a time limit.

"I remember back when we started the brand and launched a product run right around Christmas, everyone told us that for the holiday period, we should order three to five times as much product as we thought we'd sell. We didn't have the cash for that," he said.

The two friends sat down and had a serious conversation.

"How willing are you to go through with this?" they asked each other.

They were both determined to push through and decided to put $80,000 on a credit card with an 18 percent interest rate. They knew that if this didn't go right, they'd go bankrupt.

"That's when I found out how strong I was and how bad I wanted it," Marvin told me. "It turned out to be the best thing I've ever done. I finally feel like I've accomplished something all on my own. To me, that's priceless."

7

Step Five:
Launching Your First Product

When Matt and I first started growing Sheer Strength, we loved to walk around bodybuilding shows and fitness conferences, just to see what kinds of products were being talked about.

It was fun to walk up to booths that were offering samples of pre-workout drinks, take a sip, and say to each other, "Ours is better!" It was a great way to spy on the competition and also to get product ideas. Looking back, those were some of the most fun days I've ever had in business.

One day, while walking through one of the conventions, we saw a bunch of people lining up for free samples. That was a normal sight, of course; companies gave out free samples of their products to generate buzz.

But this was no ordinary line. This line of taste-testers wrapped all the way around the convention hall, even interfering with some of the other companies' booths! There were *hundreds* of people in line for a free sample of something. It was like an amusement park with everyone waiting for the most popular roller coaster to open.

I wondered if maybe The Rock was at the other end of the line signing autographs or something. (Fun fact: Matt and I always dreamed of partnering with The Rock—Dwayne Johnson—at Sheer Strength. We did meet him once, but it never materialized.)

Overcome with curiosity, I turned to someone in line and asked, "Hey, what's this line for?" He pointed up to the ceiling. There I saw the logo of a company I had never heard of: Quest Nutrition. In an instant, I became fascinated with this company.

It would be easy to think that Quest Nutrition *always* had a line of people waiting for it. It was just a few years into existence, and it was already the best-selling protein bar *ever*! I would later discover that Quest did $500 million in sales by its fourth year in business. That type of growth is amazing, but it didn't start out that way.

I became so obsessed with Quest Nutrition that I invited the founder, Tom Bilyeu, to speak at the Capitalism Conference a few years later. Tom told me that he started out by making the products himself in his own kitchen. He was hand cutting them on his own! Tom didn't even have a clear "launch plan" in place. He would talk about it to whoever would listen, and he gave the bars out for free to athletes.

Over time, small groups of raving fans started to form. They began sharing innovative ways to eat the bars. For example, if you heated it in the microwave and mushed it into a circle, it became a cookie! And if you broke the bar up and put it in a thick protein shake, it tasted like cookie dough!

This small, "hungry" group of buyers quickly became known as Team Quest. Every time Tom wanted to do a product launch or a product test, he would release it to Team Quest first. That way there were raving fans ready to buy it the day it was ready.

While Team Quest started as a small, ragtag team of superfans, it evolved into a powerful group of buyers. That passionate audience took Quest products to the gym, to the office, and eventually onto the shelves of nearly every retail chain in the United States. That small, passionate group of buyers put Quest on the map and led them all the way to a major acquisition. In 2019, Quest sold for a cool $1 billion.

Gee, I thought to myself. *Wouldn't it be nice if people would line up to buy my products?* And that's exactly what can happen to you when you do a proper product launch.

That First-Sale Feeling

The excitement of your first sale never goes away. I've launched dozens of times, and I still get excited every time I launch a new business. I still get that first-sale feeling!

At this point in the twelve-month process, after stacking the deck, there's no turning back. Understandably, there's some doubt and fear.

You're wondering if any of it's going to work—if even one person is going to buy what you're selling.

Believe me, when people do start buying (and they will), it's the most validating dopamine kick you can imagine. That first-sale notification pops up, and you think, *I cannot believe this is actually happening*. It gets even *more* amazing to see the names of people you don't recognize buying your product. *People other than my mom actually like what I made!*

Your friends and family buy your product because you've been documenting it on social media and because people you've tagged as micro-influencers are buying and supporting your product, which is a great feeling. But it's an even better feeling when complete strangers start buying your product.

That, my friend, is a real customer—somebody who found you through some sort of advertising mechanism. That advertising mechanism could be as simple as seeing someone else posting about it on Facebook, or maybe they found you by searching Amazon.

When you see that new, unrecognized, unfamiliar name, you'll grin. You'll look at your partner, or your mom, or your dog, and you'll say, in a whisper at first, "I think I just made a *real sale*."

That's when you're really in business.

Every Single One Matters

In this stage of the process, every sale is vital, and every social share or review is a potential game changer. It's your job to ensure that the momentum doesn't die after those first, exciting sales. It's your job to keep stoking that fire, and every inch gets stretched into a mile. That means winning over every customer, going above and beyond to your followers, and earning every review.

One thing I've learned from my time with Gary Vaynerchuk is that every single person matters. Every comment you reply to can create a fan for life, and every customer who sings your praises can get the attention of the next major domino. Gary appreciates every share and every purchase from his audience.

If a man beloved by millions is willing to get his hands dirty at the beginning of a new business, thanking his followers and going the extra mile for his customers, then you should expect the same from yourself.

One slip at this stage of the process can undo much of your progress. One nasty review or one faulty product can set you back for months. That's why keeping the good faith of your customers and followers is so crucial at this stage of the game.

If that sounds exhausting, take heart in the fact that the snowball builds quickly; for example, one retweet from the right person can bring in ten new customers. One video testimonial can be turned into an ad that puts you on the map. One podcast mention can signal thousands of new superfans to pay attention to you.

Every single step forward matters at this stage in the process.

It's crucial to keep stoking the fire during and after launch. Since you've stacked the deck, the odds of success are in your favor.

If you've built up buzz before launch, then the first few days will result in consistent sales every day. You will be excited, busy, and scared all at the same time. After the initial launch buzz dies down (usually two weeks after going live), you will likely see a normal "pullback" of about 50 percent.

Prepare yourself for this dip in sales. It's inevitable. You will probably freak out, but almost everyone has an initial drop in sales after the launch buzz wears off. That's where the work really starts. Stay the course.

As you fulfill your promises, going above and beyond to make your customers happy and turning sales into reviews, the snowball will start building, and you will start to grow week over week. At first, it will feel like you are scratching and clawing for every odd sale. Then you'll sell a couple of products a day. Then five a day. Then ten a day, and on and on. The dopamine fluctuations during this time are indescribable. The highs are insanely high, and the lows feel like death.

I've seen people reach a consistent, ten-sales-a-day mark within a week of their launch. I also see a lot of people who struggle right out of the gate. You'll feel tempted to think bigger if you're not seeing the progress you want. I encourage you to do the opposite: Go small. What is the smallest, simplest thing you can do to make a sale?

I used to do weekly coaching calls with small groups of twenty-five to fifty people. One day, a guy named Ken was on one of the calls talking about how he was getting his friends and family to buy, but he couldn't break through the hump. He was trying some marketing strategies to get the product to take off, but nothing was clicking.

I could tell right away that the reason Ken was struggling was because he was thinking too far out. He wasn't trying to go from one sale a day to ten sales; he was trying to go from one to 100. Ken thought it would just magically happen if he'd done all the steps in the process.

"Ken," I said, "I'm going to give you an assignment. Your job is to come back here next week with ten reviews on your product. I don't care how you do it, but come to the call next week with ten reviews on your product."

I knew that "get ten reviews" was a small enough task that he could figure it out. I also knew that if I gave him some big, complex strategy he was going to continue to struggle.

> When coaching a new entrepreneur, I have discovered that 80 percent of my focus is getting people *not* to do things. Don't build a new marketing strategy. Don't hire a new person. Focus on making sales, getting reviews, and building your audience. I had to talk Ken out of a bunch of "good ideas" to get him to focus on one thing: Make a few sales and turn them into reviews.

"Do whatever you have to do to get those reviews," I said. "If you have to order pizza three times a day and pitch each delivery guy on buying your product, then I guess you're going to eat a shit-ton of pizza. But do not come back to this call without having ten reviews."

The next week, he waited until the end of the call before he spoke up. When it was his turn, he quietly and calmly reported on his progress: "Well, I did what you told me to do."

"Okay, great. So what happened?"

"Well, now I'm getting seven to ten sales a day from people I don't know."

The rest of the group waited for him to celebrate, but he just looked blankly through my computer screen.

"What do I do now?" he asked.

"*Keep going!*" I told him, more excited for his success than he was.

I think Ken was waiting for balloons to drop from the sky. The progress felt slow to him, but it was building. His snowball was rolling. It was just enough to get his product moving, and the momentum grew from there.

When I first got stuck at five sales a day, it felt like I was climbing a mountain with no support. It seemed like it was going to be an impossibly long journey. I recognize that you're at the base of that mountain, too. It feels like it's going to be an exhausting slog that takes forever. But when you've stacked the deck right, and your brand starts to snowball after launch, that snowball builds more quickly than you'd think—and that momentum will continue as long as you keep the momentum going.

You're in the People Business Now

I remember very well the time I got my first order from a repeat buyer. After buying one time, the same customer returned and made three more purchases. I was so curious, I felt compelled to pick up the phone and call him.

He answered, and I just launched into it. "Hey, my name is Ryan, and you bought my product on Amazon. I was just wondering if I could ask you how you found it and what you think."

"Ryan," he replied, "I love your product."

I wish I had recorded it because it would have made the best testimonial! But I'll never forget the feeling. Knowing somebody loved my brand and chose to come back to it was a game changer. That's when it truly hit home, in a way it hadn't before, that building a business is a people game, not a product game.

Many internet entrepreneurs are historically guilty of optimizing for algorithms, numbers, and machines, thinking they have to game the system somehow. The truth is you're marketing to people—*communicating* with people. When you truly understand this, your marketing will get even more effective. You will be motivated to start gathering testimonials, responding to reviews (even when they're bad), and more personally engaging with your customer. You'll see sales aren't transactions, but relationships. This is the moment it becomes real.

There's No Such Thing as a Perfect Launch

I've tried to find an example of someone who smashed their launch right out of the gate, doing everything perfectly. But outside of major brands with millions of dollars in funding, literally zero examples come to mind.

That's probably because the purpose of the launch isn't to put you on the map everywhere but just to get the wheels turning. The hundreds of people who have used my work to become seven-figure business owners have almost always started from scratch, crawled their way to the starting line, launched with moderate success, and grown from there. The launch gave them the momentum they needed to start growing.

I have a student named Anthony. His first product was a baby carrier. He went from being dead broke, working three jobs at once, having no time for his kids, to launching his first product. Within eighteen months, he was a full-time entrepreneur.

When I tell you that, the assumption I just created is that he had such a good launch that it skyrocketed him to seven figures. That's not quite how it happens. I often find that people have a misconception, believing that if they get the launch right, they'll automatically be everywhere. This idea of "one, two, skip a few, launch, you're a millionaire" isn't how it happens. The launch is still in the beginning of the process, and now you have to have sales and momentum to be able to grow something.

Remember, you're still in "The Grind."

Anthony had a fine launch, but his biggest strength was that he was methodical about the process. He had three to five products in mind. He stacked the deck. He launched one product, stoked the fire, and carefully repeated the process the same way for products two, three, four, and five.

You can't skip steps and put all your eggs in the launch basket. Success comes from executing upon every little step along the way, not just the flashiest one.

The Trillion-Dollar Marketplace

You may launch on Kickstarter or use Shopify to fulfill some of your orders, but most entrepreneurs find the best opportunities on Amazon .com. Amazon is the biggest marketplace in the world, and the company is valued at a trillion dollars. It's important to understand that the process in this book is the same no matter what platform you're on, but for a beginner there's really nothing easier or more straightforward than selling on Amazon.

As your brand builds momentum after your launch, Amazon will reward you with social proof and free customers. Once you prove that you can bring customers to Amazon, it becomes its own marketing machine, putting you in front of millions of potential buyers. You will start to rank for keywords. You might start to appear on some of their advertising pages for free. You might get a "new release," "hot new release," or "best-seller" badge, which will drive up conversions. Lastly, you will start to get reviews, which can make (or break) your brand.

One of my students, Nathan, recently surpassed sixty units a day within the first three months of his launch. How? Just by following this process. Why? Because the Amazon marketing machine saw the strength of his activities and turned on in his favor.

You've probably seen the section on Amazon labeled "frequently bought together." As your friends and other people buy your product, Amazon starts looking at what they've bought before. When this marketing machine kicks in, it shows your product on the listings of other similar products. That's free advertising.

There are a few tricks that you can use to show up more often on Amazon—we'll cover a few of them in the next chapter—but one mistake people make is allowing Amazon to determine the direction of their business. You have it backward if you're deciding what products to release based on what you think will sell well on Amazon. Build a business for your customers, and let the ease and scale of Amazon handle everything else.

The biggest opportunity of selling on Amazon is that the platform rewards *momentum*. The more momentum you can build, the more that momentum will accelerate. How do you build that momentum? Loving on your audience. Getting reviews. Engaging your customers.

Don't discount the supreme importance of speaking directly to the people buying your product. Some people think they can stack the deck with fake reviews on Amazon, bought through review farms. This ploy misses the point. You're not just trying to get sales; you're trying to build a brand. If you're only focused on manipulating the algorithm, then you're *not* focused on what matters: your customers.

This is why I cringe when people say they have an "Amazon business." You don't have an Amazon business. You have a business that takes sales on Amazon.com.

It's easy to compare yourself to other similar businesses that also live on Amazon. As a result, you will be tempted to make your pricing decisions and even your next product releases based on what your direct competitors are doing. One of the most difficult things for a first-time business owner to understand is that *competitors don't matter nearly as much as you think.*

Have you ever seen the picture of Olympic swimmer Michael Phelps seconds before he defeats Chad le Clos to win yet another gold medal? Next to him, le Clos is looking at Phelps, watching him beat him by less than half a second. The meme reads, "Winners focus on winning. Losers focus on winners."

In business, you win by going all in on your customers. If you focus on trying to "beat the winner," the best you can hope for is getting caught up in a price war, which is a race to the bottom. Play your game, let competitors play theirs, and trust the system will take care of itself.

In fact, if you're correctly executing this process, you won't even be thinking about the competition. You'll be too busy talking directly to your customers, making sure you have a damn good product, and making sure they have a damn good experience.

Don't Forget to Reorder

In this stage, you're laser focused on sales, reviews, and making your customers happy.

What happens when you start making all those sales? You use up inventory. And what happens as you go through inventory? If you're not careful, you go out of business.

Sometimes people are so excited about getting those first sales that they completely forget about reordering. Without product to sell, you're not running a business. You can't take sales, and you're not making any revenue.

You should consider reordering much earlier than you think and much sooner than you're going to feel comfortable. You may think, *I have 500 units, and I'm making five sales a day. That means I have 100 days to figure this out.*

The problem is that the minute a few positive reviews come in and sales jump to ten a day you'll only have fifty days of inventory left. If you keep doing your job, you're going to end up with only ten days of inventory left. That number will keep shrinking until it gets to zero.

That's why you want to order as much inventory as you can stomach at the beginning *and* order inventory again as soon as you're able. My strategy is to reorder as early as possible, as quickly as possible. A rule of thumb: As soon as you prove your product has life, order the next round of inventory. As soon as your launch is complete or you pass ten sales per day, start queuing up the next order.

I *know* that running out of stock is the worst thing that can happen because, as you read earlier, it happened to me. I'd like to say it only happened to me once, but it's happened in multiple businesses. It sneaks up on you.

It was like starting over again each time we ran out of stock. We had to rebuild buzz, and we also lost all the momentum we'd built. I've had products that ran out of inventory but got their momentum back in a couple days. I've also had products that ran out of stock and never regained that momentum. It's just not a risk you want to take, so have a plan to ensure that you never run out of stock.

If you *do* happen to blow through your inventory, it's okay to put people on a waiting list; you just have to perform the process again, and you *have* to communicate with your customers.

I once bought a protein cereal that I found on Instagram. After I'd ordered—and paid—they sent me an email saying it was back-ordered and would be delayed.

That's not cool.

If your inventory is on back order, tell your customers right on the sales page. This information may actually *increase* sales. Showing you have demand creates social proof, and it may even justify a price hike. If your customers are cool with waiting, you'll get the sale. If they don't want to wait, they're still likely to pay attention when your inventory is in stock again. The key is to let them make their own informed choice, so your brand isn't tainted with the feeling of a bait-and-switch.

Go All In on Your Customers

It's exciting to see sales coming in for the first time, and it's fun to start calculating the amount of money that you might make if you can sustain the growth. However, since you're in the people business now, you must avoid the critical mistake of thinking it's *all about you.*

Yes, you created a cool product, and you worked hard for this, but now your product is in the hands of *other people.* Those early customers can become raving fans that give you reviews and tell their friends about you, or they can be the reason why your business stalls out. Once you've got sales for your product, your job becomes treating those customers like gold, knowing that some of them are going to leave reviews.

This is the point where I always get a million questions: How do I get reviews? When do I get them? How many reviews do I need?

How many reviews do you *need*? Zero. Plenty of people made a ton of money before the days of reviews. How many do you *want*? Simple: as many as you can get.

There are multimillion-dollar products out there with thousands of reviews, but there are also multimillion-dollar products with only 100 reviews. Yes, more is technically better, but my philosophy on reviews is that they should *confirm* a purchase, not be the reason for it. Many Amazon sellers fall into the trap of getting more reviews than "the next guy," rather than focusing on creating great products and treating customers well. Reviews are important, but they are far less important than the rest of the formula for getting to $1 million: three to five products, twenty-five sales a day, at an average price point of $30. With those numbers, you don't need hundreds of reviews; you need just enough to get past people's bullshit detectors.

Continually contributing to the pre-launch community you built is the best way to get buy-in that leads to reviews. Continue to document the growth of your business and the impact your business is making. Continue to bring in the photos that other people post of your product on social media. Take those and highlight them to the rest of your community. By doing this you continue to build up your community.

Celebrate the reviews you *do* get. Take screenshots and post them on social media. Send unsolicited gifts to people who leave reviews. Reach out personally to people who talk about your business on social media. Those relationships will create *millions of dollars* over the long run—go all in on them.

That type of commitment and attention to your customers will foster a community that supports you, loves to leave reviews for your product, and eagerly chooses you over the competition.

Then, once in a while, you can go for the ask: "Hey, we've just launched this new product, and we've been selling for fourteen days now. We might even run out of stock at this point! But we really need more reviews, to

> Amazon's search results are highly driven by conversion rate, not reviews. Reviews impact conversion rate, but conversion rate is what matters. Here's the beauty of this: In theory, if you have more positive reviews than the next person, you'll make more sales, have a higher conversion rate, and rank higher. *However, if you have an audience that chooses you over everyone else, your conversion rate is going to be higher even if you don't have a ton of reviews.* Having a responsive audience drives up your conversion rates, which drives up your position on Amazon.

spread the word, to keep pushing this message, and to get more people into yoga [or CrossFit or sunglasses or eating pineapple—whatever your group is into]. If you have used the product, and you love it, please consider leaving us a review on Amazon [or on Shopify, or Walmart. com, or wherever you're taking orders]."

Reaching a few dozen reviews during your first few months means you have enough reviews to get to twenty-five or thirty sales a day. You might not have a million-dollar product, but you'll have enough to get to twenty-five sales a day, which is your only goal before you repeat the entire process. Remember, *all you need is twenty-five sales a day*. Keep your focus tight, and when you get to the point where you've proven your product has enough action in the marketplace, roll out products two, three, and four. Then you continue the journey to $1 million.

You might find, however, that a product launch done well takes you straight to the million.

That's what happened to my friend Cathryn Lavery, co-founder of BestSelf Co., a company that helps people become more efficient, focused, and productive—in short, their best selves. Cathryn wasn't intending to start the business she did; it came about as an unintended result of scratching her own itch.

"At the time, my partner and I had our own businesses," she said, "and we started an Amazon business on top of everything. We didn't care at all about that Amazon business—we were selling random stuff, salt and pepper shakers, nothing that mattered to us. We were spread way too thinly. We were just looking for a framework to help us get everything done. We both wrote things down in Moleskine notebooks, and we liked to nerd out together on how we'd plan our days out. Eventually we realized that we could design our own productivity framework into something much more beautiful and functional. I designed it, Allen made a prototype, and we decided to launch."

Cathryn immediately wanted to launch on Kickstarter, but Allen disagreed. "He wanted to do a product launch formula, but I wanted to do Kickstarter, so we compromised and did a product launch that turned into a Kickstarter.

"Crowdfunding is incredible because there's a time limit. People see something they want—your product, or the idea of your product—and they see a clock that tells them *we need this much money by this countdown or you're not getting this thing you want.* Kickstarter also has shoppers who just back products on the platform. They have 15 million backers, and more than a third of those are repeat backers who come back and back and back to promote products."

Product development for Cathryn, like any other brand, was a long journey with a lot of changes. "We listened carefully to what our customers were saying. We gave journals away for free and took feedback on how it worked for users," she said. "When people get to be a part of development, they feel ownership over it, and they feel part of the success of the company."

Cathryn also stacked the deck with an email list she'd been compiling for three months, through content she'd been putting out on Medium.com. When launch day on Kickstarter came, they had the incredible luck of getting tweeted by Arianna Huffington as a boost to their name recognition.

Their Kickstarter for the BestSelf Co. SELF journal was funded in a scorchingly fast twenty-two hours. Part of the success was how they priced their funding levels to get Kickstarter's platform boost. "The Kickstarter algorithm prefers number of pledges over total amount pledged," Cathryn said. "So, for instance, if you have ten pledges of $500, and someone else has a thousand pledges of $5, you've raised the same amount of money, but the other company will have gotten far more attention. We used this to our advantage. We had a *one-dollar* reward level on our project, and it skyrocketed us onto the platform."

Early-bird rewards are also a huge hack to get more exposure. "The secret to funding fast is to set up early-bird rewards that *equal your funding goal*. People love getting rewarded for getting in first, and you get funded fast, look successful, and the algorithm loves you. We set it up so we only needed 200 early backers to hit our whole goal. We got it in two days. It's not that many people."

Kickstarter's organic traffic is a huge boost, which is why Cathryn and Allen put so much focus on getting momentum on the platform. One-third of all backers on their project were organic hits from people just browsing Kickstarter—eyeballs BestSelf Co. didn't have to do anything to get.

After the launch on Kickstarter, they put a "Preorder" button on the Kickstarter page, to which they were running no traffic, doing no extra work. Cathryn looked at the analytics a few days later and realized that the sales were three times what they were doing on Amazon in an entire month.

She called Allen and told him she couldn't bring herself to go back to the Amazon business and that she wanted to focus on BestSelf Co. He agreed.

"Great, we'll shut that business down," she said.

"Um, no," he replied. "We'll *sell* it." (No need to burn the house down on the way out the door.)

They went all in on BestSelf Co. and their Kickstarter campaign. Then Cathryn and BestSelf Co. got noticed by Daymond John, of FUBU and *Shark Tank*. BestSelf Co. went from mid–six figures to a million-dollar business in seven months, and that scaling had nothing to with Kickstarter. "We expanded our product range," she said. "We realized that the people who would buy their journal would buy other things to help them with productivity. We remembered watching *Shark Tank* and thinking about some of the businesses we saw—*that's not a business, that's a product*. We never wanted to be that, so we've been focused on diversifying ever since."

Cathryn's story demonstrates that if you have a great product, you are good to your customers, and you stack the deck toward a great launch, you eventually hit pay dirt, even if it's not in the way that you first imagined.

Halfway to a Million

At this point in the process, I like to tell entrepreneurs that they are halfway to their first million. They *never* believe me. Never. So, allow me to take a moment to tell you how far you've already come: *You are halfway to your first million.*

"How could that be?" you ask. "We just started taking sales for our product! I am not doing half a million dollars right now!"

At the moment, that may be true, but you'll be *shocked* at how fast the snowball starts rolling at this point. Your journey so far has been making decisions, getting your product ready, and taking an order. You've been in The Grind. Now we enter The Growth period, where your sales start to compound. While everyone is different, many entrepreneurs get to their first million just six months from this point.

That means that you might be halfway to your first million after all.

A few months ago, you hadn't even begun your journey. Maybe you didn't even know what you wanted to sell. Now, you've launched, you're taking sales, and you will soon be getting repeat customers and referrals, too.

You *can* actually build a million-dollar business.

I've seen people pace $1 million after one or two products quite quickly. They go live. Then within three or four months they have 100 sales a day, which means they've crossed that $1 million threshold.

It can happen that fast, but everybody starts at zero. Everyone starts by doubting themselves. Everybody wonders if it's going to work. If you stick with this process, stay devoted to your customers, and watch the power of compounding returns take hold, you can build a million-dollar business, as hundreds of my students have. You might even build a billion-dollar business.

But wait, forget a billion dollars—how do you get those twenty-five sales, every single day? Keep reading to find out.

Entrepreneur Spotlight: Kevin Pasco and Jeremy Sherk

Kevin Pasco and Jeremy Sherk co-founded Vancouver-based Nested Naturals in late 2013. The company launched in the summer of 2014 with two products: Luna, a natural sleep aid, and a Canadian maple syrup.

At first, Kevin and Jeremy planned to sell health foods as well as supplements—but building a brand around both maple syrup and sleep aids was proving difficult. After looking at the sales numbers, they quickly decided to focus solely on supplements.

They bootstrapped the company with loans from family. From his mother, Jeremy got an initial $10,000 loan that went into up-front costs—mainly purchasing inventory, but also for label design and building the company website. Once they began to grow, Kevin's mother loaned the company another ten grand.

Kevin and Jeremy were focused on one guiding mission for their products: quality ingredients. They wanted honest, transparent products that were natural, organic, and non-GMO. No artificial ingredients, ever. This would become the core of their branding—even if they had no idea at the time.

The first sale of their Luna sleep aid happened the first day it was put up on Amazon. Kevin and Jeremy's reaction to a single sale? They were *ecstatic.*

"*Holy shit! Someone actually bought the thing that we just worked seven months on!* That's what we kept saying," Kevin told me. "Even though we'd obviously been working toward that goal, to have it actually *work* seemed crazy to us."

The climb to greater sales was slow at first because the product didn't have a built-in audience and no advertising was put into promoting it. The partners just threw Luna up on Amazon and their website, taking it one day at a time.

They had a lot of help in the beginning. Jeremy joined my small mastermind group, which helped remove the unknown. It added to the good foundation of knowledge Jeremy had from being well versed in internet marketing, online business, and marketing in general. He went into Nested Naturals prepared to do the work, to do whatever it took to make it successful. And with that mindset, success came more quickly than he planned.

It was that ethos and mindset—and staying true to their values—that helped make Nested Naturals what it is today, generating fans and customers who supported the brand.

As they grew, Kevin and Jeremy experimented with different ways of building a social audience: They offered coupons, put a URL on their product bottles, and did anything they could to drive customers back to their website. When they got customer information or got them on their email list, they personally followed up.

One of their biggest early problems was running out of stock, which happened half a dozen times. The partners were only able to order as much product as they could pay for at the time, which led to overselling—all part of the growing pains of a bootstrapped business. Negotiating terms with suppliers was tough, and it was even tougher when inventory that was supposed to last two months sold out in half that time.

Despite these growing pains, things got better and moved faster as the company continued to iterate through repeated sales cycles. Eventually, it had enough cash reserves to order as much inventory as needed. "Three months in, we had a lot more sales than we'd anticipated," Kevin told me. "We were getting probably one or two dozen orders a day."

The company generated a million dollars in revenue the first year, mostly from sales of Luna. By the ninth or tenth month, sales had reached a couple thousand dollars a day.

Kevin and Jeremy found themselves in an odd, relatively rare position: They'd always wanted to have a brand with multiple products, but Luna did so well they couldn't keep up with its growth at first, much less launch other products.

"We realized we had to completely shift our mindset to get the company on track," Jeremy said.

The partners had originally intended to split net profits in half. They realized their business would never grow if they didn't reinvest what they made, especially since they didn't want to take on outside investment. So they buckled in for a lean journey. They each took

$2,000 a month out for the first year—just enough to barely survive. They put everything else they had into launching more products and making them work, even if it meant a year of living like monks.

The company's second product was Super Greens, a greens powder used to make nutritional drinks. They put a lot of focus on label design to establish the Nested Naturals brand and turn it into a company offering a variety of natural supplements. The approach, which was probably more labor-intensive than absolutely necessary, was for each product to have its unique branding, label, and colors. Each product was like its own brand, with a different look and feel, essentially. Doing different designs for different products got people's attention.

Down the road, however, this became a problem. People thought each product was from a different company. Even people who knew the partners thought Nested Naturals had started selling for other companies. A switch to a unified brand had to be made.

Kevin was afraid there would be customer pushback on the change, but there wasn't a single complaint. "The lesson we learned there is that no one micro-analyzes and overthinks branding more than a company's owners," Kevin said. "Branding is important, but your customers aren't going to sweat it as much as you do."

It wasn't until the company was doing $2.5 to $3 million a year that the partners decided to build out an office and hire employees. They wanted to do what they needed to do to grow bigger and faster. Traditional retail supplement brands generally have up to 500 products, and they were still only selling ten.

A former-competitor-turned-friend, who was also the first person the partners met in my mastermind group, gave the partners some great advice: "You can't do it alone."

Kevin and Jeremy started hiring. They discussed but decided against a remote team, opting to set up office space. "Having everyone in one place makes for better communication and culture, as well as greater employee investment in the company," Jeremy said. "It was the right move, but the costs were huge."

They tried to keep exorbitant Vancouver rents at bay by setting up their office in a hundred-year-old building, rather than in one that had just been built.

Nevertheless, the company plateaued during the first year after opening its office doors. Sales didn't increase at all. Kevin attributed this to a loss of focus. "We were all over the map that year," he said. "*Should we go into retail? Wholesale? Sell on Facebook?* We needed to get back to basics."

Once they refocused on their core competency, selling natural supplements on Amazon, the company started growing again. Now, three years later, they have grown to four times the size, pulling in a million dollars in revenue each month, with a staff of fifteen, in addition to several contractors who work remotely.

According to Kevin, there are things you can and should do when starting out that can't be done once you get bigger. You can test things out, change your branding, and even change your name. "Focus on getting things right when you start out so that you can then scale smoothly, as opposed to growing as quickly as possible as early as possible," he said.

It's equally important to make sure you have someone to handle inventory by the time you expand your line from one item to ten. This could be a part-time contractor at first, as long as they have the right experience. And, when starting out, don't just chase after revenue. A lot of things can start to break and go wrong once you begin selling more. When you're properly set up to scale, you can focus much more exclusively on selling more and more product.

It's important, too, to be careful once you start to succeed. "You start looking at ways you can spend money to grow the business," Jeremy said. "That's when you're going to make mistakes if you're not careful."

Once you can afford it, you start feeling there's a lot of help out there to take advantage of, but that's not always the case. "We went down the wrong road with influencers in particular, thinking, *OK, let's throw ten grand at influencers and see what happens. Of course, it's going to work,"* Jeremy said. "It was probably the biggest mistake we ever made. We got maybe $100 total back in sales."

What Kevin and Jeremy have discovered is that the best way to grow their business is to stay as lean as possible. With rare exceptions, they've resisted trying to buy their way to growth. They've focused on earning their growth by being as strategic as possible and really thinking issues through.

Kevin and Jeremy are still 50/50 partners and are as excited as ever to be running the company. They believe there's a lot of growth to be had. Each quarter is a fresh quarter, bringing new, exciting initiatives. They have an amazing team in Vancouver that oversees the nuts and bolts of the business, so they're less hands-on than before, but they're still fired up for the business. With more personnel, things move a bit more slowly, but the business is still nimble and adaptable. Even today, things change at a rapid pace.

Jeremy is just excited to be a part of it. "In the years I've been running my brand, a lot of my peers have started and sold companies, maybe even multiple times," he said. "But Kevin and I were never looking for a quick buck or a quick exit."

They believe they can reach new levels with this business, which will ultimately create a bigger exit down the line—though they don't have a timeline for that. As long as their hearts are still in it and they believe there's more success on the horizon, they're still 100 percent invested. In fact, instead of looking to be acquired, they're interested in investing and acquiring other companies. There are many different pathways in the entrepreneurial game. The key is to get going, according to Jeremy and Kevin.

"Winners start and move toward something," Kevin said. "Losers are paralyzed by inaction."

8

Step Six:
Growing to Twenty-Five
Sales a Day

In the wake of the 2008 economic crash, women and men in their twenties watched the corporate life they'd been sold come crashing down. As a result, aspiring entrepreneurs across the globe sat unfulfilled, chained to desks. The economy was flat, and the "old way" to success had collapsed, which stirred entrepreneurial desires among millions of young people itching to go out on their own.

One of those twenty-somethings was Aubrey Marcus. Like most hustlers, he tried his hand at a few entrepreneurial ventures, and he threw things at the wall to see what would stick. His first attempts: sex toys and hangover supplements.

Neither gave him success or internal fulfillment.

"I wasn't ready," he said, looking back.

Although his attempts didn't lead him to the freedom he sought, they did show him how to create a product, how to sell, and how to advertise. The process also helped him network with others who could help him along the way. That's what led him to a lunch meeting with Joe Rogan.

In the early days of Joe's podcast (now downloaded more than 200 million times per month), Aubrey advertised his sex toys on the show, becoming one of Joe's biggest sponsors.

"I asked Joe what he was into," Aubrey recalled. "And he said, 'I'm really into nootropics right now.' I told him that I would create the best in the world."

> Aubrey is a perfect example that success often *follows* major failures. Failure has a way of opening new doors that you didn't see before. Even if your first attempt doesn't go the way you want, it can pave the way for your big breakthrough.

What he didn't tell Joe was that he had *no idea* what a nootropic was. But he promised Joe that he would develop the best one in the world.

Aubrey was soon down the product-research rabbit hole, reading studies and testing ingredients, until he ultimately formulated the brain supplement Alpha Brain.

He gave some of the newly released Alpha Brain to Joe, who loved it so much that he agreed to partner with Aubrey on the new project, named Onnit. As a new owner, he also agreed to talk about it on the podcast. As a result, Joe brought Alpha Brain to his millions of subscribers on a weekly basis. The product quickly sold out, and Aubrey had to scramble to order more inventory.

Once the product was back in stock, Joe talked about it on the podcast, and it sold out again. This cycle continued until the company raised a small amount of money to keep up with the growth.

There was no vision for an empire; it was pure entrepreneurial drive. "I was just desperate to make something happen," Aubrey said.

Before long, Alpha Brain was the best-selling brain-enhancing supplement ever. It created a category all on its own—natural nootropics. The company, however, was based on the success of just one product. The company was growing, and the profit margins were high, but Aubrey knew he needed to release more products if he wanted to be a real brand.

"It wasn't until then," Aubrey explained, "that I had a vision for what I was doing and why I was doing it."

Onnit soon released New Mood, a serotonin booster made to calm down the brain and help to manage stress, and Shroom Tech, a blend of earth-grown mushrooms.

Then the company started selling kettlebells. And battle ropes. And medicine balls. Then food, protein powder, and nut butters.

The company went hard into podcast advertising, and it worked well for them. They gained national exposure, and it wasn't long before their t-shirts were seen in gyms all over the country. Then they *opened* a gym.

Instead of settling as a brain-optimization company, Aubrey sprinted full-throttle into becoming a total human optimization company. That included brain, body, and mind. Today, the Onnit headquarters in Austin, Texas, is buzzing with jujitsu classes, a full cafe, and more than 100 employees. They continue to be mentioned on the Joe Rogan Experience and many other podcasts, and they have a raving fan base around the globe.

Think about a series of products that serve the *same person*: *That's the power of a brand.*

Welcome to The Growth

Few people understand how powerful it is to take an idea from scratch, bring it to life, and make a sale. This is why I say entrepreneurs are the most powerful people on the planet; we literally make things up, make them real, and sell them to other people.

Proving you can take an order for a new product validates your idea. It proves it's real. Then it becomes your job to turn that into a machine that now creates *predictable* sales.

Your entire focus in this stage of the process is to create a stream of sales that regularly churns out at least twenty-five sales per day of your product. You do that by continuing the momentum you created by going all in on your customer: getting excellent reviews, responding to every comment, thanking your customers, connecting with influencers, and continually stoking the fire on a one-to-one basis. Doing all this will get you the reviews, exposure, publicity, and word-of-mouth advertising you need to hit the twenty-five-sales-per-day mark.

When you have a consistent twenty-five sales per day, you have a machine that can be applied to *more products*. At that point, you will release multiple products into the machine, and your business will surge past 100 sales per day, giving you the million. Yes, it can happen that quickly.

But first, we need to build that machine through The Growth. To get there, we need a process to turn a few customers into many.

How Big Can You Go?

When Matt and I first started selling our Sheer Strength products, one of my coaches asked me, "How big do you want the business to go?"

I'll be honest; the first thing that popped into my head was: *What kind of a question is that? Huge, obviously. Astronomical. World-obliteratingly massive.*

But I came up with a concrete answer. "A hundred sales a day," I said. "That would be a million-dollar business."

"What are you at now?" he asked.

"Five sales a day."

This was way back before Amazon was the behemoth it is today. This was also before automation tools and "influencers" were a thing; we did most of our marketing by hand. We called our customers. We talked to our friends, asked them what they thought, and begged for a review if they liked it. We did whatever we could to get reviews, and we celebrated every time a new one came in.

A hundred sales a day sounded like a pipe dream to me at the time.

No one comes out of the gate with a consistent stream of sales; it has to be built.

It's not uncommon to start with twenty to twenty-five sales a day during launch, only to see them come to a screeching halt once you squeeze every drop of juice out of your launch lemon. To keep that initial momentum going, you need reviews, testimonials, and good old-fashioned advertising; you're going to have to stoke the fire again and again for the next few months—and then strategically launch your follow-up products.

Getting to twenty-five sales a day is not super difficult; the *prep* to get there is. The good news is you'll have completed most of that by this point. From here, every inch forward creates a compounding return because you begin to experience repeat customers, you have a list and a process, and the whole operation starts to become a machine. Without this prep, however, you can get stuck on how far you are from the magic number and lose hope.

There's no algorithm for going from five to twenty-five sales a day. It's about building relationships with people, building trust with your customers, and building awareness in the marketplace. That's a brand.

When Matt and I were doing our own customer support with Sheer Strength, grinding it out and doing whatever we needed to do to get a review, we were totally lost. Calling customers is putting oneself out there in a big way, and it was scary. But that's also part of being an entrepreneur.

We were just willing to outwork everyone who tried to get in the game at the same time as us.

One of my employees once reflected on those early times. She said about me, "When I started working with him, I thought he was this entrepreneur who had all the answers to everything. Then, about a year ago, I realized that Ryan has no idea what he's doing."

Okay, that's a *little* harsh.

It's also basically true.

We are all winging it in life, and in business, to some extent.

We all think everybody else has it all figured out—and, believe me, *no one* does. At best, we're all competent at a few things and guessing our way through everything else.

You don't know what's going to happen when you release a product to the marketplace. You don't know what's going to happen when you call a customer. You *do* know that, at some point, you're going to get hateful comments on Facebook, and you're just going to have to get over it. You can ignore it, or you can play with it. Consider having fun with it; after all, it's a sign of success.

You will get a negative review, and it will hurt. It will make you want to quit. It will also hurt your sales. It's all part of the process. Look at it as data gathering. If you're too afraid of a few haters to build up a Facebook group, you're *really* going to suffer when it comes to growing the business past five or ten sales a day.

When I was in college, I planned on becoming a pastor. My professors in college prepared me to be ready for criticism. Sure, they meant while we were talking from the pulpit, but products aren't that different. Not everyone is going to like you or what you put out into the world. Someone will always be upset over something you said. It just comes with the territory.

That's not to say that every call I made to a customer ended in angry tirades or tears. Occasionally they'd be pissed, but nine times out of ten, people were blown away. Even the people who angrily asked, "Why are you calling me?" were taken aback a bit when I responded with, "I'm the founder of the company, and I just want to ensure you had a five-star experience."

That little touch—showing that I was already on the phone, genuinely interested in hearing about their experience—was enough to tip the scales.

Addicted to Feedback

There may be no formula or magic potion that guarantees sales growth, but I have found certain milestones do lead to a bump in sales. For example, you will see a major bump when you cross twenty-five positive reviews. And you'll see a bigger bump when you cross the 100-review mark because that means you're the real thing. There is something about seeing 100 people approve your product that crosses the bullshit detector in people's brains.

Those first twenty-five to fifty reviews can be enough to get you over the twenty-five-sales-a-day mark. A hundred will almost certainly do it; every market is a little bit different, but that's when you have enough in the marketplace to be legit, which often leads to a big spike in sales.

Again, everybody wants a formula for how long it takes to get more sales and to hit those milestones, but it's just not predictable. You just have to do the work. The first time I launched a product, it took me about three months to get to twenty-five sales a day. Now I can do it in about fourteen to thirty days because my customer list is bigger, I have thousands of repeat customers, and my process is more dialed in. You'll get there, too.

When a customer purchases your product, you can follow up with him or her in one of two ways. One option is to reach out and say, "Hey, I hope you liked the product. Could you please leave us a review?"

Pass. She has better things to do, dude.

The second option is to say, "Hi, Natalie. Did your order arrive on time? I just wanted to make sure it got there when it was supposed to."

That's a *give*. That's a deposit into the relationship bank account.

When Natalie replies that it did, you follow up again: "Great, thanks so much for the feedback. I just credited $10 to your account as a thank-you for letting me know. Is there anything else we should know about the brand? What would you like to see us release next?"

Natalie is thinking, *Damn, this company is AMAZING.*

Now you're in an exchange. You're building a relationship. You're giving the customer something they love—value, and the thrill of feeling special—but getting so much more in return. Always go for the *give*.

From there, if your customer gives you feedback or a great idea, keep going: "Hey, that's great to hear. Thanks so much for the kind words. If you feel like sharing about your experience, we would love your feedback in the form of an Amazon review." That'll do it, every time.

When a customer does leave you feedback, screenshot it and post about it on Instagram. Publicly celebrate it. Show the community that you are listening. Your job at this point is to make your customers *addicted* to giving you feedback. They don't just like your product; they love giving you reviews. They love supporting a company that's so involved in their community.

What If I'm Stuck at Ten Sales per Day?

You're going to get stuck at times.

Some get stuck around ten sales per day. They launch, get to twenty-five sales a day, then have pullback. They start thinking, *I don't know what to do now.* They start worrying about numbers and algorithms and stop being curious about the process and the people behind the purchase. They don't open up customer loops. They don't think, *Who are my people, and where are they hanging out?* Instead, they figure, *Well, my product must not be good enough; guess I better go find another product to launch.*

They spend all that time stacking the deck, building up an audience for a launch, and then they just walk away because it's not an instant success. Or, even worse, they think, *I don't understand. My product is better than everybody else's. It deserves more sales. Why aren't people buying it in droves?*

Just because you *think* your product is better than anything else on the market doesn't mean it will outsell everyone else. That's not how it works. Any idiot (and I'm not calling *you* the idiot!) can throw a product up for sale on a place like Amazon and start to get ten sales a day. And that idiot can buy reviews from cheap Chinese accounts until he or she gets caught and banned (yes, I know many people who have done this). It takes the willingness to keep grinding, being in the weeds, and cultivating a following to grow to twenty-five sales per day and beyond.

If you plateau, your temptation is going to be to think bigger. I recommend you do the opposite—go *super* micro. Remember my advice to Ken? What can you do this week to get ten more reviews? What can you do this week to blow a customer away? What can you do this week to motivate your following? Who can you contact this week who might talk about you publicly?

I have students who get a bump in sales every time they talk about their product on their own personal Facebook page because they're communicating with a different set of people. They highlight a different feature about the product, or they simply hit people at the right time. Sometimes, doing the small things for long enough is all it takes.

There *are* a few things that you can "turn up" to increase sales, though.

1. Use Amazon's pay-per-click platform. Amazon allows you to advertise within its own search results, which is extremely effective *and* expensive. You may have to spend more money acquiring the customer than you reap in profit, which means you'll be operating at a loss. However, you'll build your review machine, acquire new customers, and continue feeding the algorithm. In this case, it's better to take sales at zero profit than to take no sales at all.

2. Run video ads on Facebook, Instagram, and YouTube. If you decide to go this route, I recommend starting with customer testimonials as your first test. You can never sell your product better than other customers can. It's fast to test different messages and ads, so test several approaches until one of them clicks.

3. Put attention back into building your community. Turn your attention *away* from sales and instead put it into your community. Go back to the customer and what they want. Go back to stacking the deck. You can do a "re-launch" if you feel called to. The important thing is to return to interacting with your potential customers.

I have a student—name withheld for reasons that are about to become obvious—who is in the pet supplies business. He launched his first product and initially did well, but then he got stuck.

He's not his own target demographic, so he doesn't already know the answers to what his customers want. That's okay. You can get past that as long as you're willing to listen closely to your customers. But he stopped caring about the people behind his product, which was his brand's death sentence.

He came to me and said, "I'm stuck. How do I break out of this?"

"What are you doing now?" I asked.

"I'm focusing on reviews, I have a really good product, and I'm launching more products."

"Okay," I said. "Where do your customers hang out so that we can advertise to them?"

"No idea," he said.

"Well, you might want to start by figuring that out."

He didn't know, and he didn't care that he didn't know. He just wanted to sell more stuff.

Those people should be your sole focus as you sprint toward twenty-five sales and build your review machine. You want to know who those people are, where you can find them, how you can create the best products for them. Then, if they love your products and brand and the experience you've created, *maybe* they will leave you a review.

But, Ryan, What If I've Tried Everything and My Brand *Still* Doesn't Gain Traction?

At this point, some of you are going to be saying, "But I've *done* all of that—I've done all of the things, and I've done them well—and it's still failed to gain traction. Why, Ryan, *why*?"

Honestly, I can't tell you why—but your customers can.

If you ask them, they will tell you. Reach out to your most active followers and customers and ask for feedback.

"Do you want this? Would you buy this? Why or why not?" And then you need to *listen*.

I'm working with a company right now, and I happen to be their target market, so they sent me their product: a low-calorie fruit powder. It tasted good, looked good, and should have been a good product. But, as a customer, I had a big problem: I didn't understand how to use their product. It's not that I couldn't figure out the powder. I just had no idea when I would prefer to use this powder instead of regular, plain old fruit. ("Stir it in yogurt!" Fruit. "Add it to smoothies!" Frozen fruit. "Just add water!" Um, why?)

I gave this feedback to my contact at the company, and, instead of listening, he told me why I was wrong. He gave me a rational, intellectual breakdown of why I—the customer—just didn't understand the product.

"Dude," he said emphatically, as though if he just said it another way I would finally grasp the concept. "It *replaces fruit!*"

I still can't figure out why I'd want that.

Someday, he'll get it. He'll have a great launch because he's got a big audience. The product will sell. People will be excited to try it, and then it's going to head to the back of their cupboard, where they'll never touch it again.

If your product fails to gain traction, despite your steps to do everything right, then it's likely that something went wrong in the initial stages. Entrepreneurs are big thinkers, but they often think *too big* at this stage in the process. Go back to the customer, to the following. Focus on the micro.

Maybe you didn't get enough people in one spot. We've talked about needing to create a place that has at least 1,000 followers talking about the product. Maybe you tried one thing on Instagram, and something else on Reddit, and then a third thing on your YouTube channel. Now you have a lot going on, and it may seem like everyone is talking about your product, but you still don't have 1,000 people in one place.

I have a student named Michael who sells products for gardeners. During the stack-the-deck phase, Michael went all in on a Facebook group; he doesn't have an Instagram following, and he's not on any other platform. He just focused on building that Facebook group and now has 14,000 gardeners all in one place. He can launch whatever he wants and get all the feedback he needs. As a result, he can also earn whatever profit he wants.

What did he do to get those 14,000 leads? He created a community that was responsive and helpful, and people invited their friends. Now the group grows by hundreds of people each week without him lifting a finger. He promotes his product in cool and ethical ways within the group, and his community rewards him for it.

I'm Making Twenty-Five Sales a Day! What Do I Do Now?

First of all: *Congratulations!* You've built a machine that can support a million-dollar business.

Now what?

Easy: It's time to repeat the process. Get ready for launch number two, and then three, and then four, and then five.

In fact, you never stop repeating the process. You go back to where all your customers showed up, and you engage even more.

People often ask me, "If I do everything right, what percentage of my first-launch customers should I expect to come back and be repeat customers?"

If you did everything right, this answer is easy, too: all of them.

All those people who love your first product and who had a great experience with you and your company will come back and buy product number two. If you do this right—if you create those leads, if you talk to them and listen to them, and do all the people-oriented things we've talked about so far—you can expect return buyers.

The process for launch two is just warming up all of those previous customers so that you have an even bigger launch the second time around. In fact, it should be even easier now as there's no ramp-up process for product number two. While you worked hard and put all your time into launching the first product, product two will come more easily. You're simply engaging more with what the customers who have already purchased from you want. So, you can skip the stacking-the-deck process and double down on the people who are already there.

You're in the home stretch, really. Now we sprint to the million.

Do you remember Travis and Jenna Zigler, the optometrists I talked about earlier? Their brand is called Eyelove, and they did a fantastic job of paying attention to their customers. They do Q&As with their customers and actually listen to the questions and feedback they get. They regularly do Facebook Live events to interact with all their raving fans as well.

Their products have higher price points, but every time they launch a new product, they go from zero to fifty sales a day within a few weeks. People leave reviews, and it snowballs. That focus gave them the machine that has now built a multimillion-dollar business.

When you finally hit that magic number of twenty-five sales a day, it's time for you to start building your snowball, too. It's time to choose product two. Let's look at how exactly to do that.

Entrepreneur Spotlight: Jason Franciosa

Jason Franciosa was coming off a failed business and searching online for what to do next when one of my ads popped up on his screen. Immediately intrigued, he decided to join my community at Capitalism.com.

After learning my method, Jason dove right in and launched his company, Element 26.

Jason and his business partner, who is a doctor in physical therapy, looked at a bunch of ideas for products. In the end, they came to exactly where Matt and I had ended up with Sheer Strength: They targeted themselves as the customer.

They were both avid weightlifters. The fastener on their weight belts always failed over time.

"It was pretty obvious what product to put out first," Jason told me.

They knew that the true key to success with this product would be doing something different. They weren't alone in their struggles with Velcro. When they looked at all the biggest weight belt competitors, and read online reviews, the theme of failed Velcro was consistent and clear.

They set out to design the best, most functional weightlifting belt possible, while solving that main problem: How do you fix the Velcro?

They reached out to manufacturers and got a variety of samples. They looked at using buckles, clasps, and a clip with teeth that dug into the belt. They got prototypes of about five different solutions and tested them. They also considered what type of material they would use. The width of the belt, the shape, all of it came under scrutiny—all while sticking to their core values as a company of functional products for functional athletes. No marketing gimmicks.

They finally settled on a self-locking buckle, a slide lock that actually supports the entire pressure of the belt as opposed to the Velcro. When they launched and marketed the product, they focused on the problem their belt would solve—the failing Velcro. By understanding what their audience was looking for, Jason and his partner centered all their marketing material on the design difference between their belt and others. It helped them stand out and eat away at the competition's sales, while still keeping their prices high. It also helped shape their reputation and started to build their brand within the space.

Jason attributed a lot of his success to his product being different, and in bringing an obvious improvement to a well-used product in the CrossFit and weightlifting communities. But he also benefited from relationships with influencers.

When it comes to influencers, Jason found cold calling ineffective—unless you just want to pay for a post. "The best way is to meet people in person by going to events, having a handshake, providing some sort of value to the influencer," he said. "Especially if you can understand what they care about and make that personal connection."

It's even better if you can bring the influencers into the development cycle, which is what Jason and his partner are trying to do now. "As you build new products, the influencers give input. What this ends up doing is creating a complete buy-in once the product launches."

Influencer events are great, but going to events in your chosen market is just as important. "At the end of the day, you're selling to a person," he said. "Just because they're behind a computer screen doesn't change the fact that it's a person. How can you really know your people if you don't go to the events where they hang out and meet them face-to-face?"

Jason said they have faced some challenges—the constantly changing Amazon platform, initial design problems, and a change in packaging. The new design looked great, but their manufacturer failed to mention that with the new printing process, there was an odor. Suddenly, they started getting bad reviews about their product's smell.

Despite these challenges along the way, they went from zero to $10,000 a month in two months. They consistently grew for a year and a half before focusing on launching new products.

"Find one product that works, get the cash flowing, and then, as quickly as possible, start testing new products. Double down on products that work great and get rid of products that do not," Jason said. "If I could have a do-over, I'd be more aggressive with the timeline than we were. As soon as the business is self-sustaining, and there's no out-of-pocket expenses, you should launch the next product—roughly when you're selling $10,000 to $15,000 a month on a single product."

Jason and his partner both had full-time jobs when they first started the business, so their process dragged out a little bit because they were not 100 percent working on the business at the start. As a result, it took them a little longer than twelve months to get to $1 million; instead, they were at a million in twenty-four months. Jason left his job, working full-time on the business. He and his partner are finally at the point where they take an owner's draw.

"The money is great," he said, "but honestly, it's the freedom, and all the people I've met and built relationships with, that makes this fulfilling for me."

9

Step Seven:
Build a Million-Dollar Brand

Remember Dave Asprey's fancy coffee?

When Dave launched his company, Bulletproof 360, in 2013, it quickly became famous for his recommended morning brew: coffee, blended with butter and MCT oil. It was only natural for Dave to launch his own coffee brand of organic, "upgraded" coffee as his first product.

He followed up with his own line of butter and MCT oil, which helped him to establish a steady stream of revenue and raving fans. Had he wanted to have a small, profitable coffee company, he could have stopped there.

But Dave desired to be more than a coffee company; he had his sights set on becoming the go-to source for upgraded performance. Over the next few years, Dave would release everything from supplements, to sleep induction mats, to a "whole body vibe," to a $15,000 five-day retreat.

Of course, it would have been impossible for Bulletproof to do this right out of the gate. They had to crawl before they could run. But with a raving fan base that supports all his products, Bulletproof has the ability to release whatever products Dave is inspired to create.

Just like Bulletproof, your brand will be defined by the products that you release. Your first product was your gateway; it made it easy for your audience to start their journey, and to choose you as their guide. But to create a real brand, your follow-up products must lead the customer to the next stage of their journey. These follow-up products will ultimately define what your company becomes; they will also lead you to cross your first million.

Stage Three: The Gold

When our first Sheer Strength product hit twenty-five sales a day, Matt and I were beside ourselves.

It was a major milestone. At the same time, we knew it was just the beginning. If we were going to build a million-dollar business, our math told us that, at our price point, we would have to sell four products at twenty-five sales a day to get there.

After hitting twenty-five sales each day consistently, our product leveled off. You're always going to hit a plateau. Luckily, that plateau is a milestone itself: That's when you'll know it's time to release your second product.

After we released product two, sales started to climb quickly, much faster than they did with the first product because we already had a built-in audience of customers willing to try our second product. In fact, our second product started out-selling product one within just a few weeks.

Then something weird happened. Once the second product hit twenty-five sales a day, the first one jumped up from its plateau and began doing fifty sales a day! Sales that were previously flat had now doubled! The second product actually bumped up the first product.

Previously, we had feared that the two products might *take sales away* from one another, but they were actually feeding one another! Why did this happen? There were a couple factors at play. First, we had repeat customers coming back for more and buying additional product. Second, customers started buying them together as a bundle. They saw that we offered two products, so they just bought both. There was a network effect, a sort of natural referral process, happening. And finally, some people had followed us during launch but had not purchased; they were following our journey, and when they saw us release more products, they joined our fold by placing orders.

Beyond that, two products started to juice up Amazon's internal marketing machine. The algorithm was working for us, introducing people who were interested in one of our products to the other one. Potential buyers would see "these two products are frequently bought together" and "customers who saw *this* also saw *this*."

We thought we had hit the peak at twenty-five sales a day; we thought that we were already at the top of the market. We were wrong.

That product quickly bumped to fifty sales per day, and then more. By the time we sold the company, that same product was doing more than 300 sales a day.

This is the snowball effect. Product two's launch is boosted by the success of product number one, but then sales from product two also bounce back and boost the first product as well. Back and forth, back and forth, snowballing into more sales and greater profits.

That's why this stage of the process is "The Gold." It's when your hard work finally starts to pay off. It's when sales start to increase exponentially, and every product you release creates a multiplier effect. New customers start to find you organically, and the million is so close that you can smell it.

You have proven that you can take a product to twenty-five sales per day, and now you need to do it a few more times. Remember the formula: Three to five products at twenty-five sales per day is a million-dollar business.

Your task is simple: Release more products as quickly as you can comfortably handle, without getting distracted.

From One-to-One to One-to-Many

My mentor, Travis, once told me something that most people don't realize: Everything you're doing in business is really just audience-building.

When you release that first product, you're building an audience of customers. You have to do all the things we previously talked about: build relationships, reach out to influencers, and kill them with kindness until they voluntarily give you feedback and reviews. When you release the second product, your audience is already primed and responsive, and they will reward you. They bought from you once, and they are likely to do so again.

At this point, your systems start to break because *you are the systems.* Even the most well intentioned business owners may have trouble keeping up with the number of customer inquiries, the comments, and the number of customers coming in the door. That forces you to make some changes. You want to continue doing all that outreach you were doing pre-launch, and continue to build up your consumer base, but now, instead of talking to people one-to-one, you're talking to *many* people at the same time. You're engaging with an audience and still building those same connections, but now you're doing it at scale.

You're talking to your audience as a whole rather than to each person individually. In addition, you now have a network of fans that can help you with promotion. If you haven't already, start taking screenshots of positive reviews and sharing them with your audience, or get your customers to do video testimonials and run them as ads on Facebook. Every customer testimonial can be used as content for your audience, and every post of someone holding your product or making a video review can become an ad or a social media post. Your customers are creating social proof on your behalf, rather than you having to create it all from scratch. Using it at scale is powerful.

Every influencer that you previously connected with is watching your growth. If your first launch went well, and you're getting positive reviews, then it validates other people's decision to take a chance on you. Take advantage of these networks. People are highly influenced by others, so continue to share positive reviews, glowing emails, and every ounce of publicity you receive. All this will feed the pre-launch machine to set up your second product to be a hit.

Remember, the more external traffic and sales you can send to Amazon, Kickstarter, Walmart, Shopify, or wherever else you are taking orders, the more that those big machines reward you. It is more important than ever to continue to document the build-out of your company, talk about the decisions that you make as a team, and keep the attention of your followers and customers.

Developing Product Number Two

Choosing what to roll out for your second product should be an easy decision, but many people screw it up.

The biggest mistake people make is trying to pursue a second niche market with their next product. Your second product is always the answer to this question: *What's the next thing that my first customer would want to buy?*

To know this, we go back to the group of products your customer *already buys.* If you don't know what your customers want next, then you entered the wrong business, or you got so wrapped up in your first launch that you lost sight of the brand. That's why it was so important to identify the three to five products that your ideal person might want to buy. If you've been doing the work, you already have a list from which to choose.

The order of products naturally flowed within my yoga business. Our gateway product was a yoga mat. What's the next thing they would want to buy? We put out a yoga towel. We followed that with a yoga block, then a foam roller. We could have kept going, but parties interested in acquiring us came knocking on our door, and we sold the company.

Many people are tempted to follow up their first product with add-ons, additional colors, or new sizes. That is fine, but it's *not* a second product. Accessories are *not* new products; they create incremental gains at best.

It's important not to waste a good product launch by releasing a "1A" version of your first product. Your second product should create as much buzz as the first or you won't get the multiplier effect that can double your company's sales.

Think of it this way: Your customer is on a journey. They are the hero in their decision to lose weight, or become an author, or be more eco-conscious. Your job is to make it easier for them to overcome the challenges they will have along the way. Supplemental products don't help them overcome their challenges; they just help them consume your first product more. Consider a laptop. When you buy one, you have the option to purchase all sorts of accessories, like a case or a keyboard cover. They are supplementary products, not new concepts. Apple would have a hard time being a trillion-dollar company if they only sold one product with add-ons.

Selling incremental changes doesn't get people lining up at the door, waiting for your next product to go live.

What Kind of Company Are You?

Your second product can define the type of company you will be for the next year. Recall that Onnit set out to be *more* than a brain supplement company, and Bulletproof *more* than a coffee company. As a result, both had to change their product lineups as quickly as possible.

If you get stuck releasing products that are too similar to your first product, you might get pigeonholed. You might plateau and end up being smaller than you could be.

That's why it's important *now* to decide what type of company you want to be. If you did your job at the very start, and you understand your customer, then this part should be easy. Your company exists to help your ideal person along his or her journey, after all.

My friends Cathryn and Allen had tremendous success when they released their BestSelf journal. It took off like a lightning bolt, selling millions of dollars' worth of product. But when it was time to come up with a second product, they struggled. How do you follow up a first-ever-at-bat home run? They were already selling inserts and cases for their journals (note: supplemental products), but they didn't have an idea for a killer second product to release.

One day, while we were chatting, I asked a simple question of them: "What kind of business do you want to be?"

If they were a journaling company, then their next products would be simple: more journals, fancy pens, and, well, that would be about it. But I had a hunch that they wanted to be something different.

After talking for a while, they hit on the answer: It's not about journaling; it's about *productivity*.

That realization opened up a whole new realm of ideas. Instead of just selling journals, their job was to develop products that helped their customers become more productive. Shortly after, they released their second product, called Tempo, the world's first adjustable hourglass, designed to help you organize your time and stay focused—and it happens to be a beautiful object to look at, too. It's a tool that fits in perfectly with BestSelf Co.'s overarching brand concept and aesthetic. That made them more than a journal company.

Second-Product Pitfalls

It's rare for a second product to hurt you, but I have seen entrepreneurs release new products that, for whatever reason, never really took off.

If you've done the work to build an audience, it's extremely rare to have this happen on a first product. But it could happen on a second product if it doesn't live up to expectations. Or, if your second product doesn't bring your customer further along their journey, then they're unlikely to line up as eagerly as they did for your first product.

Many times when entrepreneurs launch their first product, they're still trying to find their voice as a business. Sometimes that voice and identity changes. It's not uncommon for people to be targeting one audience and find that the raving fans are a different demographic than they expected, which happens when they either don't know their audience, or their interests change. I cannot count the number of entrepreneurs who had a successful first product, only to realize they had no passion for the audience they targeted. When that happens, go back to redefining your ideal person.

One of my students, Jonathan, came to me when he was selling about a million dollars per year in makeup bags. He had done something extremely special: created fantastic products that people absolutely loved and crossed a million dollars in sales. He was also miserable.

Jonathan joined The Backroom, which is my small group of mentoring students, some of whom I personally invest in. As a result, we spent many hours talking about his business and what he wanted to accomplish.

He had no interest in selling more makeup bags. His plan was to grow the company a little bit more, sell it, and move on. But I noticed something interesting about Jonathan: He lit up like a Christmas tree when he talked about new ideas. He came to life when he talked about the suitcase he wanted to launch or the journals that he wanted to create to help people achieve their goals. He even enjoyed talking about his ideas for creating and selling closet organizers.

One day, I found the thread in his thinking when I asked him: "Jonathan, what gets you excited about all these new products?"

He sighed. "I guess," he said, "that I just want to help people declutter their chaotic brains."

That was it!

It wasn't about makeup bags or suitcases—it wasn't about the product at all! His brand was about the *result* that his products created: decluttering his customers' chaotic brains.

Jonathan's brilliant design was the thing people loved about his makeup bags. The bags had a special place for *everything*! And the suitcases he had been designing made it simple for you to remember to pack *everything*! They had a special place for each item, which made it easy to pack for your next trip. The closet organizers he had been sketching followed the same idea. It was like each product took just a little bit of your crazy neuroticism and put it into a nicely organized place.

I got excited as I realized his target customer wasn't just women with messy purses, but also *me*. I would love to have a suitcase that was so well organized that it made my life just a little bit simpler.

If Jonathan had kept releasing more and more makeup bags, he would have always been a makeup bag company. But once he identified what he wanted his company to be, he realized he had something more: His brand existed to organize the chaotic world. That set off a tidal wave of product ideas.

When you identify exactly what you want your company to be about, then your job becomes simply developing the products that make it easy for your customers to carry out their journeys. You may not hit a home run every time, but each product will serve a purpose within your brand.

Deciding *what* to sell next is important, but it's even more important to decide *when* to release it. It's common to release products too quickly, without giving the customer time to breathe.

Speaking onstage is one of my favorite things to do, and I love to do Q&A after a live talk. Once, during the Q&A session at SellerCon—a conference for Amazon sellers—one attendee asked, "I'm launching ten products right now. What would be your suggestion on how to do that without overwhelming my audience?"

"Simple," I said. "You don't. You can't. Your audience will absolutely be overwhelmed. *Don't do that*. Sell one at a time."

He pushed against me, but I stood firm. Don't launch ten products at the same time. Launch one. You will make more money and maintain more momentum. To get the snowball going, you need to reach twenty-five sales a day, and it's difficult to do that when you're watching and pushing ten products.

It's also just poor optics. Ten products on Amazon with only a handful of reviews each isn't as powerful or trustworthy as one product with lots of glowing reviews. Do one thing extremely well, and then do it again.

Competition and Unique Value

I consult with a lot of businesses that have released a successful first product but don't know what to do next. This is often because instead of trying to serve their customer base, they are getting hung up on analytics and surface-level metrics.

When Matt and I launched Sheer Strength, there were no product research tools that estimated how much money a product would make on Amazon. I believe this ignorance was a strategic advantage for us.

I cannot tell you how many times an entrepreneur had a successful first product but then struggled to act on releasing the second product because the data scared them. Don't fall into the trap of making decisions based on volume, or trying to get a piece of someone else's action; instead, do what is best for your own business and your customers. There are enough slices of the pie for everyone. You don't need to dominate a market; you just need to get each product to at least twenty-five sales a day. And remember: Always default to serving the customer, and let the numbers fall where they fall.

When I asked Tom Bilyeu, the founder of Quest Nutrition, about competition, he shared a unique perspective. Quest bars were the first of their kind to market, and their product was an immediate hit. But within a few years, there were so many other "paleo" protein bars on the market that it was hard to keep them all straight.

Tom told me that when you bring a new product to market you have about eighteen months before people start copying you. He said to enjoy that honeymoon phase, but never forget that they're coming for you. The solution is to constantly be innovating and staying one step ahead.

In many cases, competition can actually benefit your brand by building awareness. When yoga was just a small niche a few decades ago, more brands on the scene benefited everybody because it created awareness of the practice and got more people interested.

If Dr. Oz came out with a supplement I already sold, I would be *pumped*. He would bring in a huge audience of people already primed to see the value of that product. A lot of them might buy it from him, but some of them would buy mine.

Keep in mind that the company that you think you're competing with may end up acquiring you. Do your thing, and let them do theirs. If other people invade your space, keep innovating and keep serving your customers. At the same time, be open to collaboration or competition: *cooperative competition*. After all, you're both spreading the same message.

Tom put it well: "Our company mission isn't to make protein bars," he said. "Our mission is to end metabolic disease. And if another company comes along that does it better than us, we would support them."

A few brands that I advise have similar, but not duplicate, products in the same space. They will often cross-promote their noncompeting products to each other's audiences. Their audiences benefit, and both companies see a boost in sales.

Customers will switch products, but they don't often switch brands. A brand is just outsourced trust. It's an expensive risk to try something new, which is why it's so hard to get a business off the ground. Once you build that trust and validation, people will continue to buy from you. Someone else promoting awareness about your products only helps your brand. Stay in your lane, and don't let their decisions determine where you go as a company.

The Big Picture

Brands do well when one product puts them on the map, and its success leads to future purchases. Most of the brands that we love have one flagship product, and it paves the way for future products. People come to you for your BestSelf journal, your Bulletproof coffee, or your Quest bars. While they're looking around at your brand, they end up buying the other stuff you sell.

This is partially why audience is so important; the ability to put firepower behind each product launch is invaluable.

However, your "hero" product, the flagship your brand becomes known for, may not be the first product you release, or even the second. I've seen examples in which the first product did fine, the second did fine, but the third just took off. It's impossible to know which product will most resonate.

Always keep in mind your central goal: to build a million-dollar business in one year. To do this, you need three to five products, each earning twenty-five sales a day, at a $30 price point. That's it. Your only goal after launch is to get to twenty-five sales a day, which unlocks the next product, which then unlocks the next. Keep focusing on that momentum, and the snowball will roll all the way down the hill.

Entrepreneur Spotlight: Paul Miller

Paul Miller started his business, CozyPhones, from absolutely zero. A previous business failure had left him completely broke, and he was healing from a major physical injury. In a moment of desperation, Paul threw his hat at one more business attempt.

Four years in, CozyPhones did $6 million in sales.

"Honestly, your videos changed my life," Paul told me recently. "I never would have started without that blueprint, and I never would have made it to where I am now."

Years ago, Paul had used sleeping headphones—a soft headband, with headphone speakers inside. He used them to listen to podcasts when he couldn't sleep (one of those podcasts was mine). But the headphones weren't well made and often broke.

As he was looking for new ones one day, an idea came to him: *I could make these better myself.* He found generic sleeping headphones and ordered a small batch of them. Then he set to work tweaking the product, making the sound quality better, adding more colors and patterns, and improving the build quality.

He put the product up on Amazon, and it took off.

But this wasn't the real genesis of CozyPhones—at least not where revenue is concerned. The biggest inspiration for his product came while Paul was doing a product photo shoot. The photographer put his headphones on her little ten-year-old. "That was my moment of revelation," Paul said. "I thought, *Wow, this could be good for kids—they're comfortable, kids can lay down with them, they stay in place, and they're great for travel.* But I knew kids would want more than just the typical colors. I thought of what my kids would want, and the wheels really started turning."

His daughter helped him create his first design—a green frog version of CozyPhones. It took off even faster than the original product he'd put on Amazon.

"Little kids don't like earbuds or big, bulky headphones," he said. "In addition to being comfortable, CozyPhones are volume-limited, so it's safe for their ears. Kids loved them, and parents loved them, too."

Discovering this niche market made all the difference, and Paul ran with it, creating a bunch of animal themes—unicorns, bunnies, foxes, and cats.

Then, out of nowhere, Paul's product took off with an audience he'd never expected.

CozyPhones were a hit with kids with autism and sensory processing disorder (SPD). At the time, Paul didn't even know about SPD. When he realized the benefit, he started joining Facebook groups for autism and SPD and offering free samples. He asked families to use his product with their kids and give him feedback.

"The thanks from the parents of those kids felt incredible," Paul said. "I felt like I wasn't just selling stuff. I was helping families."

CozyPhones still sells a lot of adult sleep headphones and continues to expand this category as well with Bluetooth and different styles and colors. But expanding into the child audience made all the difference.

The next big step was moving into licensing. Paul now works with Nickelodeon; CozyPhones makes exclusive character headband headphones for Paw Patrol, Teenage Mutant Ninja Turtles, and other franchises.

The worst obstacle? "Copycats," he said. "From day one, they were there. A hundred popped up overnight selling my exact product."

As a result, he has a patent pending on CozyPhones. When he gets his patent issued, he plans to deal with the competitors. Right now, he is constantly innovating—always trying to make it a little bit better than the other person's.

He believes it's critical to get out of your tunnel vision of how a product could be effective. "I had no idea where my product was going to hit, and I was really surprised by the ways people used their CozyPhones. I never would have imagined the audiences I'd reach," Paul said.

He advises trying to think outside of the box in terms of audience for the product. Can you modify the product and make it work for different groups? For example, he's recently created a sweat-wicking CozyPhones headband for runners.

Paul scaled up quickly, and he plans to keep scaling with the licensing relationships he's building. "I thought in the beginning being a million-dollar business would be amazing," he said. "I believed it was possible, but I never dreamed that within three years I'd do over four and a half million, while still working from home."

10

Step Eight:
Getting to $100k per
Month and Beyond

Building a million-dollar business in twelve months is a great accomplishment. It's like a rite of passage.

I'm proud to have helped hundreds of entrepreneurs hit that goal. But two of my friends, Josh Bezoni and Joel Marion, make that accomplishment look like chump change.

When they started BioTrust, they set out to create a health and fitness company that would leverage the relationships that they had built over the years, allowing them to serve their customers in a way no one else was.

They didn't do a million dollars in sales in their first year, however. They made more than *$100 million* in their first twelve months.

Their small team did not use Amazon, retail stores, or any of the "traditional" ways of marketing, either. They took all the orders on their own website, and most of their customers came from old-fashioned email marketing.

I invited Joel to the stage at the Capitalism Conference and asked him the obvious question: "How the heck did you do that?"

Joel's answer was simple and unsexy. It also flew in the face of every piece of advice that most business owners follow.

His secret to hitting $100 million in just twelve months: be willing to *lose money*. "If I know that I am going to make thirty dollars from a customer after ninety days, then I am willing to spend twenty-five dollars up front to acquire them and nurture them," Joel said.

Most people would give up if they didn't make money within thirty days, he told me, but he looks at the long-term relationship with a follower and a customer, rather than the short term. If you know that you can get the numbers to where they need to be over the long term, then it's okay to lose in the short term.

Most of the entrepreneurs that I know have a serious fear of losing money in the short term. If they cannot spend $1 to make $2 right away, then they fear loss, bankruptcy, and certain death (to risk being a bit dramatic). But if you know a customer is going to stay with you for the long run, then it makes sense to "lose" in the short term. That's how Michael Dubin acquired so many customers for Dollar Shave Club, and that's how Joel and Josh built BioTrust.

If you want to build something, you must be willing to actively acquire customers.

"If I can spend more money to acquire a customer than my competition, then I am going to win every single time," said Joel.

Marketing, like everything else, is building a committed relationship. But most people see it more like a one-night stand.

Back when I was really trying to break into the entrepreneurial circuit, I went to an event for a bunch of internet marketers. One guy there, the most prominent information marketer in the space at the time, was flapping his gums about how well he was doing. Other people crowded around to listen, presumably just flocking to bask in his infinite wisdom. I was there, too, but I elbowed my way to the front of the group so I could piece together his whole strategy.

"Look," he said. "The way it works is there are eight of us with email lists, and we take turns saying who is up. When you're up, I'll promote for you. We get you to the top of the rankings, and then we move on to the next person."

I nodded. "So it's basically a big circle jerk?"

Other people laughed, and he just looked at me over his drink. "Yeah, basically."

I was pretty sure right then that this was not the business I wanted to be in, but it taught me a valuable lesson: *If you have access to the people who control the audience, you can make any product win.*

Smart entrepreneurs put their money into customer acquisition and building a long-term relationship with them. If a customer stays happy, they will continue to pay you money over a long time.

This type of thinking doesn't make sense if you *only* sell yoga mats, or one product of any kind. If you spend $30 to sell a $30 yoga mat, you're not going to make much money. But if you have yoga blocks, towels, mats, teas, clothes, and meditation cushions, then you will happily spend $30 to acquire a $30 customer—because they eventually come back and buy more. When you have several products in your arsenal, it's time to start thinking like this.

Doing this separates you from the rest of the pack *fast*. When you can create your own exposure, you can launch product after product, putting you at "seven-figure status" in no time. That's why this stage is called The Gold.

Everybody Needs Somebody

To build a million-dollar business, you need three things:

1. A place to take sales, whether that's Amazon, your own store, Kickstarter, or a combination of all three
2. A stacked deck with a small following to whom you can launch products
3. A way to expose your products to new audiences

When I started, email marketing was my main way to get eyes on a brand. That still works. Today, however, you have more options; potential buyers hang out in pockets, so they are easy to target with ads. They also tend to follow specific influencers. The purpose of advertising is to drop your bait into a hungry pool of fish, giving them the opportunity to strike.

You can accomplish this via paid advertising, or you can accomplish it through building relationships. You can either pay to show up in front of your potential buyers, or you can network with the people who control the distribution. Both strategies work, and both *require* work.

For some, connecting directly with influencers—minor celebrities who have thousands (or sometimes millions) of people following them—is a holy grail. *If I could just get one of those big celebrities to talk about my product,* they think, *then millions of people will know about it, and I'll be rich!*

That *does* happen, but not like people think.

Yes, Onnit had Joe Rogan, and The Honest Company had Jessica Alba, but in those cases, the influencer is an owner in the business, not a spokesperson. Building a relationship like that can take years. It is no way to efficiently build a seven-figure business.

On the other extreme, there are some businesses that will happily pay social media celebrities to talk about products. But little to no *trust* is passed on in that exchange, and it rarely has the impact expected. In my opinion, paying an influencer to talk about your product is a fast way to lose money and get frustrated in the process.

However, there are ways to advertise and create relationships that can drastically improve your sales when they are done correctly. This chapter will show you how to get tons of exposure for your brand, without going broke. You'll discover how to find distribution, how to choose advertising platforms, and how to network with influencers.

For the purposes of your goals, you won't need to develop a complex marketing strategy or spend a ton of money on advertising; our singular goal is to cross $1 million in sales in twelve months, and we can be very direct in accomplishing this. The fast lane to get to $1 million is going straight to the people with *influence* and leveraging the trust that they have with their audience to create your own following.

Start in the One Spot Your Audience Already Hangs Out

The best audiences to target are people with the same buying behaviors as the people who will buy your product.

I have a podcast, so I maximize my exposure by going where the podcast subscribers are: other podcasts. To build my audience, I needed to network in the podcast pool. One mistake a lot of people make is trying to bring people from one platform over to another. You don't need to waste your time trying to convince people to go other places; you just go where they are.

At this point, most entrepreneurs ask, "What's the best platform to advertise on to increase sales?"

Wrong question. The right question is, "Who's already buying products like the ones I'm going to launch, and where are they hanging out right now?"

If you penetrate that platform, you'll have all the buyers you can handle for the next year. Sometimes it's easier to ask, "Who does my target person follow?" Then you can just look that person up and see where they create content. Find that one anchor influencer and his or her halo of influence. Then find similar influencers and platforms to that individual.

The most impactful platforms, in order of sales impact, are podcasts, blogs/email lists, YouTube videos, and social media. The key to all of this is getting *endorsed traffic*. In other words, when someone endorses your product, sales rise. Networking with the leaders of podcasts, blogs, and YouTube channels can get all the early adopters you'll ever need.

For example, consider what is commonly referred to as the "intellectual dark web." This small group of podcasters and YouTube hosts consists of writer Sam Harris, podcaster Joe Rogan, YouTube host Dave Rubin, and editor Ben Shapiro, among others. When author Jordan Peterson released his book *12 Rules for Life* in 2018, it quickly got the attention among members of this media circle, and they scrambled to feature him on podcasts and interviews. A year later, the book had sold more than three million copies.

Similarly, when Silicon Valley entrepreneur Andrew Yang decided to run in the 2020 US presidential election, few voters had heard of him. However, his approach got the attention of Sam Harris, who featured him on his podcast. That put him on the radar of Joe Rogan, who also hosted him. That created a series of opportunities for exposure. A few months later, Yang was polling ahead of some of the major candidates, and he qualified for the Democratic debate stage in July 2019.

What does all of this mean for you?

It means that if you can cross into the "good ol' boys" club that controls the media in your niche, your brand can take off *scary* fast. The "hack" for this is to reach out to influencers who have around 10,000 followers—not 1 million, not 10 million, but just 10,000 and above.

That means that you will be reaching out to mid-tier podcasts, under-the-radar blogs, and modestly sized YouTube channels. They are big enough to impact sales, but small enough to say "yes" to little ol' you.

Over time, you'll work your way to your niche's circuit, and their audience can become your audience.

So how do you find them?

Start by searching hashtags on Instagram. Then subscribe to your niche podcasts and notice who is regularly getting booked as a guest. Subscribe to relevant YouTube channels and keep a pulse on the "water cooler" conversations happening in your space.

I also recommend that you use SimilarWeb.com to find blogs and websites that are impactful. You can enter the URL for a big influencer's website, and it will spit out other websites with similar demographics. Make a list of ten people with around 10,000 to 50,000 followers with whom you can talk about your product. Who are they, and how can you leverage that relationship once you've built it?

Remember: You don't need every influencer in the space talking about you. You only need a handful of people talking about you. In this particular case, a handful can change everything.

"Hold up," I can hear you saying. "I don't want to be appearing on a bunch of podcasts, and I definitely don't want to be on someone's YouTube channel."

That's totally fine. You never need to appear on a YouTube channel or do a single interview in your life to create a seven-figure business. But you do need to know the people *who do*. No matter what your business ambitions, you need to know the people who control the media in your niche.

You open relationships with them by making deposits into their accounts.

Make Relationship Deposits

Once you know where your audience hangs out, and you've identified a few key mid-level influencers, the next step is to make connections with those people. I call this step "making deposits into your relationship accounts."

Too many people try to make withdrawals from bank accounts they've never made deposits in. Just like a real bank account, that's not how relationships work. Withdrawing from an empty bank account *puts you in debt*. The same is true with relationships; a relationship must have an equal flow of currency between two accounts, if not a positive balance in your favor.

But how do you get there? Well, you have to start making deposits. You get there by *giving*.

Every day, I get Instagram messages that ask, "Will you mentor me? Will you do this for me? Can you teach me how to get rich?"

These used to annoy me so much that I would sarcastically respond, "Dude, I don't even know who you are, so yeah, obviously I'll drop everything and mentor you." Today, I just block them.

I've said this before, you *always* want to go for the give instead of the ask. If you go for the ask, you're an ask-hole. Don't be an ask-hole.

Relationship building takes time, so the sooner that you start making deposits into other people's accounts, the sooner that you will have a positive balance from which to make "withdrawals." If you don't yet have a product with positive reviews, then your job is to give without expectation. People will indeed take a look at your brand, and, if you can't show a product with a track record, they are unlikely to take you seriously. It doesn't mean that you can't start making deposits, it just means that they won't talk about you until you have generated your momentum; only then will they willingly share it with their followers.

You start by giving them an obvious, easy way to say "yes." The smaller the yes, the easier to get, and you start the relationship there.

Get the Smallest Yes Possible

How do you get the attention of someone you have never met, who has no reason to pay attention to you? After all, you can't make a deposit in that relationship bank account if you don't know the routing number. Like a good friend of mine, The Godfather, said, you do it by making them an offer that they can't refuse.

You go for the smallest "yes" possible.

If you can get them to say yes to anything, you open up a conversation, which opens up more opportunities to put deposits in the bank account.

What's the easiest way to get someone to say yes? Answer: Give them money.

The easiest way to meet new people is to do business with them. And the easiest way to do business with people is to become a customer.

In fact, that's my favorite way to open a conversation: "Hey, I'd like to give you money."

There aren't many statements that grab attention better than that one. I go on: "I love your podcast and would love to advertise on it. Will you please send me a rate sheet?"

If that person takes advertising, then you have immediately opened up the conversation. Just like that, your foot is in the door with influencers that you want to meet.

I have paid speaking fees, donated to charities, offered to do bulk buys of books, and sponsored podcasts and events, all because I wanted to build a relationship with someone. It's some of the best money that I have ever spent.

If you don't want to pay for advertising, or you don't yet have the profit margins to do it, then find other "gives" that open doors. I once saw on Twitter that someone I wanted to meet was visiting Austin, Texas, and she was craving some tacos. I offered to hire Postmates to deliver tacos to where she was staying. That's a true story.

My friend John Ruhlin takes a different approach. His company, Giftology, sends amazing custom gifts to people he and his clients want to meet. In fact, that's how he and I met; one day, I opened the mail, and a signed Cleveland Indians bat and ball were in there. There was no note, no return address—just a gift. In fact, I had to *hunt down* the sender! John has since been to my home, and we have attended Indians games together. He gave without expectation, and now, when he calls, I answer the phone.

Give first, and watch how fast your network changes. Offer to share an influencer's content or to make an introduction. Offer to email their content to your list. The minute you give rather than ask for something, you stand out from the crowd. Most people are ask-holes.

Look at that list of ten influencers you identified, and start to position yourself. What can you offer them? Quote them, reference them, comment on their content, or ask them if you can feature them in front of your audience. Find out where they are giving a keynote and how you can buy a VIP spot. What charity are they into that you can sponsor? Get creative, and you can easily make a relationship happen.

Maybe you want to give your product away to their audience. "Hey, I saw that you completed a marathon. I'm sure there are a lot of people who have been following that journey. Can we send twenty-five samples of joint supplements to your audience, on us?" It's another deposit. When they complete that marathon, publicly congratulate them. Make them look good to *your* people.

You don't have to be The Godfather to make an offer that someone can't refuse. An offer is as simple as doing something that is impossible to turn down.

Do I Have to Be Best Friends with a Celeb?

If you build a business around an audience, you most certainly have a competitive advantage. For some, that means building a business around one core influencer or celebrity.

In fact, my friend Brian Lee only launches companies when he has an A-list to partner with. His first billion-dollar venture, LegalZoom, was built around the famous attorney Robert Kardashian. That connection allowed him to get unlimited PR, and the company eventually grew to what it is today. His second big success was ShoeDazzle with Kim Kardashian. His third was The Honest Company with Jessica Alba. Now, he has Art of Sport with Kobe Bryant. He builds the team, raises the money, and brings on the celebrity, and he creates billion-dollar companies. He is an amazing entrepreneur.

However, it is the influence that matters, not the celebrity.

For example, an acquaintance of mine paid Jennifer Lopez to act as a spokesperson for a supplement company for which he worked. She's a great choice, but she was just a hired face. She had no buy-in because she wasn't a customer of that company. She didn't use the product; it was just her face all over it. Was she putting it out to her audience? No. The company quickly folded.

Genuine enthusiasm for a product, the truthful and organic endorsement to their followers, is what makes influencers more powerful than spokespeople. An influencer *actually uses and believes in the product*; a spokesperson just slaps their name on the box.

An audience can smell a celebrity cashing a check from a mile away. For a celeb's involvement to actually influence an audience, they need to be a customer, too—and their endorsement is word-of-mouth advice, not a gig.

Just like all forms of advertising, influencers are not a surefire road to gold. They *are* a surefire way to get exposure, but your product and your brand still need to stand on their own. Even when people manage to find big influencers to enthusiastically talk up their products, if the product isn't right for their audience, the audience won't budge.

For example, a friend of mine was an investor in EXO Protein, which is a protein made out of insects (crickets are the protein of the future!). They sponsored everyone from Tim Ferriss to Dave Asprey to talk about the company. Every time the product was mentioned by a big influencer, sales would spike, but they would inevitably fall again. Unfortunately, the market just wasn't ready for cricket flour, and the company did not last. Even the best marketing in the world won't make people buy a product that they do not want.

For the purposes of hitting your first million, networking with celebrities is an unnecessary waste of money. Your goal is to get a small but raving group of people to discover your product, love it, and share it with the next tier of influencers. You just need to light the spark.

You don't need millions of people to know about your product—in fact, that would probably break your operations. You only need twenty-five sales a day. Go small, and the million is right around the corner.

My Influencer Said Yes. Now What?

Some influencers are going to politely (or not so politely) say no. Others might not respond at all. But eventually one or more will say yes, and you will have the opportunity to sponsor them, work with them, or send them product to review.

Now what?

I highly recommend using their exposure to create a communication channel of your own. In other words, bring their followers into your world and treat them well, and they will become buyers over time.

Even in today's chaotic, noisy world, the highest converting communication channel available to you is email marketing. If you could only build one "sales" channel outside of Amazon, I would suggest that you build an email list of customers that you nurture over time.

For example, if I sell keto coffee creamer, and I sponsor a podcast, I would *never* write the ad to say, "You can find Klean Keto Koffee products on Amazon." That would be a huge waste of an opportunity. I want the ad to say, "Klean Keto Koffee has over 1,000 reviews on Amazon, and you can save 10 percent when you go to KleanKetoCoffee.com/10."

That way, I can track how many visitors come to my link, and I get their email address before they go over to my store.

I do this when I sponsor an Instagram influencer, too. Rather than pay the influencer to talk about us, and then hope and pray that we get sales, I tell them to send their followers to follow *us* on Instagram to get a discount. Then, we put a discount link in our Instagram bio or in a swipe-up story. Most companies just throw money at influencers and hope that it results in sales, but that's a big mistake. Bring them into your area of control first.

When you get in front of an influencer, and they're talking your products (whether for free or because you paid them), make a point to make them look good for doing so: interact with the comments on those posts, thank them publicly, or send them a care package of your products. Over time, some of those relationships will remain transactional, where you keep paying somebody to talk about you, but you keep them at arm's length. Some will become real relationships, where you're actively engaged in that person's following and adding value to their life. Some will become superfans of your brand, and they will talk about you incessantly for free.

If that influencer posts about you in any way, *screenshot that shit.* That screenshot can become an ad. It can become content. Or you can put it away for a future launch.

Continue to kill your influencer with kindness. I once talked about one of my favorite books, *Clockwork* by Michael Michalowicz, on one of my podcasts, and he immediately sent me a care package with a bunch of his books in it. That's a deposit in my relationship account! In turn, I took a picture of the goodies and posted it to Instagram, which drove sales for his book.

The goal is to consistently have more deposits than withdrawals in your relationship account. Gary Vaynerchuk calls that *leverage.* Showing kindness and asking for nothing in return builds up goodwill, and people almost always want to repay a kindness.

The Snowball Gets Bigger

Most people overlook the power of micro-influencers, but they can create a cascade of effects that will completely change your brand.

Once you've opened relationships with influencers who have 10,000 or so followers, you can leverage those relationships to an influencer with 25,000 followers. Just four relationships with 25,000-level influencers gets you in front of an audience of 100,000 people!

That's when the floodgates open. Send them free product. Pay them if you need to. Start the snowball rolling any way you can. You may progress from people with 50,000 followers to 100,000 followers or even a million followers, but honestly, you don't have to. You can continue to network your way up, but there's more than enough business to be had right in that range. This is all you need to start to consistently see sales in the hundreds per day; each new product will amplify all your existing products, too.

This is when you start to flirt with having a million-dollar business.

To this day, if I had only one place to advertise, I would spend time networking with other "audiences" (an audience may be a person—a blogger or YouTube personality, for example—but it might also be a group or an organization, too) and paying them to talk about me on their podcasts, YouTube channels, blogs, and social media. It's that effective, and it alone can take your brand past the seven-figure mark and beyond.

After this, there's only one thing left to do: scale the brand, or sell it.

To Most People, You've Made It

Let's do some quick math. What's 100,000 × 12? Yup. 1.2 million.

When you get to this stage, and you're on the step where you level up to $100,000 in sales per month, then you're on the cusp of "making it" in most people's eyes. You're on the cusp of a million-dollar business.

This is the home stretch. It's a long home stretch, but home plate is in sight.

Throughout this process, you've seen the steps in this process build to this moment—a million-dollar business. You've done the work, and you're about to reap the big win. This next stage is a huge jump up—not just in revenue but also in your mental state as an entrepreneur. When you start flirting with $100,000 a month in sales, lots of things change.

First of all, you're running a million-dollar business. Just take that in for a moment.

From the outside, everyone is going to think that you're hot shit. You're a millionaire. You have a seven-figure business. You have everything figured out.

But, if you're like most people, you'll still be hustling, figuring it out, and wondering "when things will change."

One thing *is* different, though—and this is the big one—your brand is now big enough to be scaled or sold. You've proven your brand makes money. You've proven it has an audience and buy-in from influencers. You've proven it can grow. Now, you can decide if you want to scale this into a multimillion-dollar business, or if you want to sell it. A business selling $1 million–plus per year can theoretically be sold for a seven-figure payday. Conservatively invested, that money sets you free for life.

If you're like most people, though, this is just the beginning.

When Sheer Strength hit $100,000 a month in sales, it took us by surprise. We'd been so focused on all our marketing activities and carefully stacking the deck for every product launch that we hadn't actually looked closely at our revenue in a few months. When I did check in on our numbers, I recalled a conversation Matt and I had about four months earlier, when we launched our first product.

"How would you feel about hitting $100k a month?" I'd asked Matt.

He thought I was joking, so he answered sarcastically. "No, Ryan," he'd said. "I don't want to make $100,000 per month."

He thought I was kidding because, at the time, it seemed like such an incredibly distant dream that we couldn't imagine what that would be like.

But I insisted: "No, Matt, I'm serious. I want to set the goal of hitting $100,000 per month in sales, and I want to work toward it."

He kind of shrugged. "Okay," he agreed. "Honestly, I'd be happy making an extra $2,000 per month."

That is what made us great partners. I was the dreamer, and he was the pragmatist.

In reality, it took us almost exactly twelve months to go from start to $100,000 in sales a month. Twelve months to a million.

Here was the crazy thing, though: When we got there, we didn't feel any different. I think I'd imagined that I'd wake up as a millionaire and start perceiving the world in a new way—colors would be brighter, food would taste better, people would be nicer, and I'd . . . I don't know . . . *feel rich.*

But I didn't. At that point, it was just a number, the next step in our business. I realized then that it had only been a number in the first place. There was nothing magical about getting to a million; I'd done it, and I knew then that I could do it again, over and over. I had a process that worked.

One Big Change: You Get Paid

When do I start paying myself? It's a question I get asked all the time and a valid one. After all, I said right in the introduction of this book that building a million-dollar business isn't a side hustle; it requires your commitment, not just of energy, but of time. So when will you start getting rewarded for your efforts?

Up until the point when Matt and I reached $100,000 a month, we were rolling every single dollar we made back into the business, reinvesting the profits to grow inventory faster. You'll want to do the same. However, here's one big change that happens at the $100,000 point: You can safely start paying yourself an income.

My students are often confused when I clue them in that they won't be getting paid by their business for an entire year. My response is simple: While the business is growing, the profits aren't your money; they're the business's money.

If you pay yourself too soon, growth stalls. If you're taking money off the table, you won't have money to build your snowball. It's that simple. While you're building out to a million dollars, that cash is worth *so* much more in the business than it is in your pocket, so leave it in the business.

At the $100,000-a-month mark, though, you can start to take some of that money off the table and put it in your pocket.

When we reached that point with Sheer Strength, I wanted Matt to quit his day job and work on the business with me full-time. He was worried about giving up his paycheck.

"How much are you making now?" I asked him.

The answer was $68,000 a year. "Great," I said. "Do you want to double that?"

That's how we decided how much to pay ourselves. I wish I could say it was more scientific or well thought out, but it wasn't. We replaced his income so that we could both be full-time in the business. Pay yourself that amount when you decide to go all in.

Revenue Roller Coaster

If you are like most entrepreneurs, then you will encounter this scenario: One month, your business makes $200,000 in revenue. You're elated. Well, but hang on: The following month, it only makes one-third of that. This happens all the time, and if it happens to you, don't be alarmed.

The question becomes, Are you still a million-dollar business?

Here's the rule of thumb: If you sustain an average of $100,000 or more for three months, you're a million-dollar business. End of debate.

While swings in revenue are common, it's much more common for people who carefully follow the process in this book, step by step, not to experience wild swings. Instead, most people will see sustained, steady growth as a result of their efforts.

If you have your systems set up for stacking the deck and releasing new products, and if you take the time to build the audience through influencer relationships, then the growth of your business will sustain itself. In fact, you get to determine when you have swings because you control the audience. Need a surge in revenue? Do a promotion. Need to boost slow sales? Call on your influencers. Product reviews are going down? Ask your audience.

The biggest swings that happen are actually *great* ones: things like Black Friday (a glorious day). You have Christmas rushes. You have spikes in attention due to well-placed podcast interviews, blogs, and influencer engagement. And Amazon Prime Day will take on a whole new meaning for you.

Here's an example of a *good* swing that can happen with your brand. Recently, I was on vacation in San Diego, shepherding my dad through a tour of the West Coast, something I'd always wanted to do. I was in his hotel room one morning waiting for him to finish puttering around in the bathroom, and I flipped on the television. The *Today* show popped up.

The show featured a panel of supplement experts talking about different protein powders, and one of the panelists casually dropped the name of one brand of which they were a *huge* fan. It was a brand that belonged to a good friend of mine.

I dug out my phone and shot him an email on the spot: *Dude! I'm watching the* Today *show and they just mentioned you!*

Five minutes later, he responded: *Woah that explains the sales I'm seeing right now! Aw yeah!!*

That kind of spike is completely random, and it might never happen to you. To this day, my friend has no idea how that panelist (or more likely, that panelist's publicist) found his brand. It's not out of the realm of possibility that this could happen to your brand—there are people whose entire job is to just sit on Google and Amazon and track rankings, note trends, and make recommendations. If you stack your deck well enough, and get enough people talking about your brand, they'll do all the work to get you in the conversation.

Operating this process well is the same as building a niche skill. You'll have to practice on your first two products to get it just right, but once you do, products three, four, and five will be where the brand really takes off—not just in recognition, but in revenue. From there, you have all the tools and knowledge you need to scale infinitely. Using the steps you've learned, you can build a world-class brand over and over. And if you build it right, other companies will come knocking on your door, ready to write you a check.

Entrepreneur Spotlight: Jeremiah Klingman

Jeremiah Klingman more or less stumbled into starting his first company, Tribe Fitness. After all, when you're just eighteen years old, you don't usually have your eyes set on building a company you can sell.

He was selling on Amazon, doing retail arbitrage to generate cash, as any young hustler would. He knew very little about making his own product, and he registered the name "Tribe Fitness" on Amazon on a whim. He experimented by listing his first product, a cell phone armband, which he white-labeled from China. His first order totaled just 400 units.

Before long, he realized how important high-quality reviews were to a brand's success. He learned that the brands who were winning had the best reviews, so he solicited feedback and gave his customers whatever they said they wanted.

Inventory arrived from China in small batches, and each batch was tweaked and further adjusted. The bands were too big for people with small arms, while still being too tight for people with larger arms. There was a lot of trial and error. He would adjust a batch one way, get feedback that the straps were still too small, and then adjust the next batch another way. They kept finessing the strap system with hundreds of tweaks, until finally it could be looped around one side of the armband if a customer wanted it looser, or around both sides if a customer wanted it tighter. At that point, the armband had stopped looking like every other armband; it had become a unique product in the marketplace.

As a result, Tribe Fitness got to the magic twenty-five-sales-a-day number in three months. However, Jeremiah knew that the top sellers in the armband market were going at a rate of a thousand units and more a day. With that amount of upside, he wondered if he could take this to the million-dollar level. The company went all in on its armbands and waited about six or seven months before launching a second product.

Jeremiah and his partner kept tweaking the armband for about a year, working to get the best possible reviews and doing split testing of various product versions to see which got the most conversions. The more reviews they got, the better the sales. Tribe Fitness managed to get reviews from 4 percent of its customers, which was about double the review rate of its competitors.

Before long, they were surging to the top of Amazon's search results, and they quickly surpassed a million-dollar run rate. Then, at just nineteen years of age, Jeremiah was passing established businesses with millions of dollars in funding. How? A commitment to product and customer experience. He went small, which helped him to beat the big guys.

What's most important in a physical products business these days, Jeremiah believes, is building an audience. "This wasn't as important four or five years ago," he told me. "Then you could start a business, get by, and even get to a million in annual revenue before you started focusing on your audience. It's extremely hard to do that now. You need to build an engaged customer base and collect their data consistently."

Jeremiah has learned that to build an audience you need to maintain focus on your core business above all. Concentrate on whatever is pushing the needle and moving the business forward, constantly keeping the pedal to the metal.

"My other advice is not to lie to yourself," Jeremiah said. "It's easy to get sloppy, substituting 'probably' for 'definitely.' Do you actually know what the customer wants and where you need to go next? Don't assume anything and really look at the numbers. Use them to understand why your business is where it is. If you have either a spike or a drop in sales, look closely at what's happening. Focus on analytics and learn to understand the numbers. Be honest."

Four years after starting Tribe Fitness, Jeremiah decided to cash in his chips and sell the company. He talked with brokers, negotiated on rates, and filled out countless questionnaires, financial records, and other paperwork.

Jeremiah had calls with prospective buyers every few days for about six months, which became a job itself. "One of my friends, who had been through the same process, said that selling a business is like doing your taxes every day for a year," Jeremiah told me. "He definitely knew what he was talking about!"

After a few false starts and a few deals that didn't pan out, Jeremiah eventually got the payday he was looking for—a multimillion-dollar check arrived on his doorstep when he was just twenty-one years old. That earned him the nickname of "the richest kid in Maine," as I referred to him on the podcast. As long as he invests it well, he will never have to work a day in his life. However, he now has his eyes set on something bigger—his next business.

11

Step Nine:
Putting It All Together

The process is simple.

It's not *easy*. But it's simple.

The beauty is in its simplicity, and that is partially why so many entrepreneurs have used it to become successful. When you strip out all the noise of entrepreneurship, success comes down to creating a great product for a very specific customer, giving them the opportunity to purchase, treating them well, and using basic marketing to amplify what's working. Then you repeat the process until you are pacing a million dollars in sales.

The hardest part is overcoming the mental noise in your head that wants to overanalyze every decision. When I speak with entrepreneurs who have used this process to build a million-dollar business, they tell me that what helped them the most was having a proven and straightforward path to hit their goals. This book has provided that, but your brain will inevitably want to overcomplicate things. That's why so much of my work with entrepreneurs is encouraging them *not* to do anything that falls outside of this process.

When you feel lost in the sauce, or when you hit a roadblock, this step-by-step process will clarify the path forward.

Stage One: The Grind (Months One to Three)

Your job within your first few months in business is to *take a sale*. Nothing happens until something is sold, and your job is to get to that point as fast as possible. You don't have to understand everything or prepare for every possible challenge, and you don't need to have a pretty website. Your packaging doesn't need to be perfect, and you don't need to listen to every person's opinion. Your job in this stage is to make imperfect decisions as fast as possible.

If you are already a millionaire, and you're waiting for your next opportunity, then you can ignore this advice. But if you desire freedom, crave success, and dream of entrepreneurship, you need to make decisions and move forward. It does not matter if your decisions are wrong. You can fix bad decisions later with new decisions.

You might choose the "wrong product." You might enter a niche that is "too competitive." You may not price your product "perfectly." But you don't know that right now, and no amount of information is going to get you to the point where you do know that. Just make decisions and move forward—progress is way better than perfection.

"Researching" is not making decisions. "Networking" is not making decisions. "Journaling" is not making decisions. Decisions mean that you are moving forward, and you are choosing what to bring forward. You can always go back and make different decisions, but you have to choose *something* to create progress.

Here's how to get out of The Grind as quickly as possible:

1. Define your core customer. Starting with an ideal "person" makes all other decisions easier.

Theoretically, you could skip this step and put all your focus into developing a great product, but you run the risk of developing what we call "the golden turd"—a great product that you keep polishing and polishing, without ever knowing who would want to buy it. If you know who your core customer is, then it is nearly impossible to end up with a turd.

As you outline your core customer, note how they identify themselves—what groups do they belong to? It's okay (and recommended) if this forces you to cut off a good portion of your market. If you are selling gloves that appeal to both woodworkers and gardeners, pick one group and target them. Your core customers will take your message to the rest of the world.

You cannot create a product for everyone. You can only create a product for *someone*. Therefore, you have to decide who that is, even if your product could appeal to more than just your core customer. Make a product that your core loves, and let them take it to the rest of the world.

2. Outline three to five products that your core customer buys. When your ideal person is starting their journey, what do they buy? If you cannot name at least three products, you either need to ask them, or you need to choose a new market. You will need multiple products to hit the million, so do not move forward if a market does not purchase several different items.

I know several people who made a short-term killing selling fidget spinners and eclipse glasses (yes, that's a thing), but they were out of business as soon as the fad faded. They were sent scrambling to find the next product. You cannot scale or sell that type of business, so don't move forward without identifying the first three to five products that your core customer buys. Otherwise, you will stay stuck as a perpetual hustler, not a real entrepreneur.

It's important to note that you do *not* need to release all these products, nor do you need to commit to each one of them. You simply need to be absolutely clear that this core customer makes multiple purchases for multiple things. You have to know that you can get customers over the long term and that you are not a onetime purchase. To do that, you will need multiple products.

3. Choose your first product. Out of the list of possible products that you outlined, one of them may stand out as an obvious "gateway product"—the purchase that leads to other purchases. If one does not stand out, then choose the one that interests you the most.

Alternatively, you may identify an obvious way that one of the products could be improved on. Is there something that your core customer doesn't like about the options for one of them? If so, pay attention. That's a sign you're onto something great.

4. Pick a place to document your journey. Sharing your progress will build an audience of potential customers, and it opens up opportunities through the network that you build. That random person who is fascinated with your brand knows an influencer, a blog, or a retailer that can radically change your journey.

Document your journey where your audience already hangs out, if possible. Otherwise, do it where you will be consistent. If your audience follows certain Instagram influencers, then start an Instagram for your audience and document the journey there. Re-share the content on your personal pages, and engage with every comment, like, message, or share.

5. Order prototypes and place your first order. Get samples from several different suppliers, and choose the product you like best. You may decide to get feedback from your audience when deciding which supplier to use. If all else is equal, choose the one with the best communication. In fact, I will pay a premium for proactive communication from my supplier.

When you have a product you're happy with, order as much inventory as you're comfortable ordering; your biggest challenge isn't likely to be sales. Instead, it will be keeping enough inventory. For that reason, more inventory is better in most cases. If, however, you are using crowdfunding to build an audience or to fund the business, you can get by with a very small amount of inventory and order the rest later.

6. Stack the deck. While your inventory is being made, you can put yourself in the best position to hit the million by building a small but passionate audience. When you have a few hundred people who are actively watching your journey, then you have enough to move the needle. You may decide to run ads to get those first few hundred fans—even $10 per day can get you there.

Line up at least ten personal contacts (friends and co-workers are fine) who represent your ideal customer and ask them to join your cause, which would include engaging with your posts and talking about your product on launch day. Give them free product and take photos of them holding it. Those photos make for great content, and they are great ad images, as well.

If possible, make a relationship with at least one audience with 10,000 followers. Remember, an "audience" may be a person, group, or organization. Any place where at least 10,000 of your core customers hang out has the potential to put you on the map.

7. Take an order. Take a sale as fast as possible. It is rarely, if ever, a good idea to delay your "get money date." Many entrepreneurs delay their launch in favor of doing more content or preparing for every possible challenge. Don't be like them. Take a sale and figure the rest out later.

When you have successfully taken a sale, you can move on to the next stage.

Stage Two: The Growth (Months Four to Six)

Once you have taken an order, your singular focus is to get your product to a consistent twenty-five sales per day. In some cases, this happens within a few weeks of launch. Other times, it can take several months. Either way, you must hit twenty-five sales per day before you move on; otherwise, you have not created the foundation that will take you to the million.

Getting there requires you to be active within your audience and to get high-quality reviews. Spend this time to go above and beyond to make your customers happy so that they voluntarily talk about you, share your work, and give you feedback in the form of reviews and follow-up sales. Continue to respond to every comment, share every photo, and post pictures of your best reviews on social media.

Here are a few things to consider during The Growth:

1. Does your audience actually want your product? If your sales are stuck, you need to go backward. Have you asked your audience for real feedback? What do customers think about the product? If they love it, but sales are slow, you might just need more time. If the feedback is less than stellar, it may be time to take a step back and rethink your product line.

2. Think small. You don't get to twenty-five sales a day by building complex systems. You get there by doing the small things for long enough. Get *one* review today. Make *one* customer very happy today. Post *every single* piece of positive feedback on social media. Make connections with small influencers. Those little pieces of progress stack on top of one another.

3. Cultivate a core group of buyers. Consider developing a VIP list, a private social media community (like a Facebook group or a Slack group), or a first-buyers list. Quest Nutrition, for example, uses "Team Quest" to test new products and be first in line for new product launches.

4. Utilize pay-per-click advertising and video ads. Advertising on Amazon is a no-brainer if you are collecting sales there. You may have to take a loss on the customer acquisition cost, but it is a no-brainer to get the snowball building. Consider making videos—even selfie videos are fine—and putting them on social media. If one of them really connects with your audience, consider running it as an ad to boost sales.

The Growth stage is where you earn your scars as an entrepreneur. You learn how to deal with customers' feedback, and you learn how to get comfortable taking sales. If you quit during this stage, you haven't earned the right to be successful. Focus on serving your customers, and this stage will fly by.

Stage Three: The Gold (Months Nine to Twelve)

Your job in this stage is to launch as many products as you can comfortably handle, without deviating from your central focus. This stage is when the snowball effect happens; the success and engagement that come with the launch of additional products will create repeat buyers and additional advertising opportunities.

The process to release these products is the same as launching products one and two. But when you launch products three, four, and five, the snowball effect doesn't just increase—it accelerates. The engagement with your brand begins to take on what feels like a life of its own; your repeat customers begin to compound, and the mentions your brand gets across social media increase.

Each product release will get a little easier and a little faster. Some of your products may only be singles or doubles, but a few will be home runs. It could be that the big takeoff doesn't happen until you've already released a few products.

While you are in The Gold, consider the following:

1. Only launch products that are multipliers. Additional colors or sizes do not count as "new products." Sometimes, they are necessary to include, but they will not have the same multiplier effect as a brand-new product. Remember that your customer is on a journey, and your job is to make it easier for them to overcome the challenges that they will face along that journey.

2. Advertise via influencers and audiences. If you can only spend money to advertise in one place, give it to influencers and other people's audiences: blogs, groups, social media pages, YouTube channels, and podcasts. Only advertise to audiences that are a direct representation of your ideal customer.

3. Make relationships, not transactions. Be intentional to create relationships with influencers and channels, instead of just transactions. Sometimes, you have to transact to get their attention, but go deeper. Send thank-you cards and gifts, and make them look cool on your social media channels.

4. Pay yourself. When you are hovering around the $100,000 per month revenue mark, you can start considering taking a salary from the company. Pay yourself enough to allow you to work full-time on the business, but continue to reinvest the profits back into the business. The business still needs the money more than you do.

5. Take strategic risks. When you have crossed the million-dollar mark, you can start to take some risks. Launch new and innovative products. Experiment with new forms of advertising. Consider debt as a resource to fund your inventory. You have proven that your company has promise; now is the time to turn up the heat.

If you follow this process, and you do it in order, you will see progress. No one can promise you that you will hit the million, or that everything will always be rosy, but you *will absolutely make progress.* If nothing else, you will have learned the process for creating a product and taking it to the marketplace. From there, your customers decide who wins. If all else fails, you know exactly what to do when the next idea or the next opportunity falls into your lap.

In my experience, the "idea of a lifetime" comes around every six months. With this process in hand, you will be ready when it arrives.

---— **12** ———

Step Ten:
The Big Payday

Mark Sisson was in his early fifties when he started blogging on MarksDailyApple.com. He had experienced his own set of health challenges and business setbacks, so he might as well share them with the world.

Modestly successful, Mark tried several businesses over his career. Now, with grown kids and entering what most would consider their "golden years," he decided to focus on doing things that he loved—namely, writing and sharing his knowledge with others.

Mark wasn't your average fifty-two-year-old. What other fifty-something has six-pack abs and can run circles around kids half his age? As a result, Mark's blogs, books, and podcasts started to catch steam.

However, it would be a full decade before Mark would launch his own products. In his early sixties, Mark created Primal Kitchen, which started as a paleo condiment company.

There were plenty of health food options, but few condiment companies that were good for you. He decided to do something about that.

Mark had already stacked the deck—his blog was frequented by tens of thousands each month. And he had connections from his previous businesses. Still, Primal Kitchen was a risk. Most people his age would have told him to slow down, keep writing, and enjoy time with his family.

Once again, Mark was no ordinary sixty-something. He launched salad dressings, barbecue sauces, mayo, ketchup, mustard, and other condiments that were all designed for the paleo community. They were beautifully targeted specifically to the paleo community, and his audience loved it.

Soon, Primal Kitchen products were in retail stores across the country, while also soaring to the top of Amazon.com.

Then, less than four years from launch, Mark made a connection with an unlikely ally—the executives at Heinz. Some saw Heinz as the enemy, a representative of unhealthy food choices. But Heinz saw the demand for healthy options, and they knew that Mark had carved out his niche.

In early 2019, they wrote Mark a check for $200 million.

Some accused Mark of selling out, but Mark saw it as an opportunity to infiltrate the rest of the world. When consumers start demanding healthy options, and those options start outselling the big boys, even "enemy competitors" have to pay attention.

That's the power of creating a great product for a *very* specific group of people.

The Exit Is Closer Than You Think

Walking into a meeting earlier today, I felt my phone buzz in my pocket. I pulled it out to see the following text on my lock screen:

Hey Ryan! I've been a follower for a while. I listened to your podcast and went to the last CapCon. With your help, I started my company last February, and today I'm about to go to market with it for $10 million. Can I ask you a couple questions before I do?

First of all, I have *no idea* how this person got my phone number.

Second of all, I didn't care. That's *exactly* the kind of text message that makes my day.

Selling your company, especially for $10 million or more, is life changing, to say the least. Heck, it's *generation* changing. I've seen it happen many times, and it never gets old. If you use the method in this book, you may find yourself in a position to one day sell a business *if* you want to. This is absolutely possible, assuming that your product is good, you've built a good business, and you have put in the step-by-step work I've taken you through.

In fact, you really make your money when you *sell*. Even after you cross the million in sales, you will still likely be paying yourself a modest salary, investing as many dollars as possible back into the business. You celebrate when you finally cash in your chips.

When you've just started a business and you're working on getting to twenty-five sales a day, I understand how overwhelming it can be to think about an exit. Just as building a million-dollar business seemed impossible at one point, so does selling a company, even *after* you've hit the million.

Whether you decide to sell your company or scale it into the next Onnit, Bulletproof Coffee, RXBAR, Quest Nutrition, Honest Company, or Procter & Gamble, you need to understand how big of an advantage you have. If you follow the process in this book, you absolutely have an edge over others—even the big companies that are dominating right now. People who have come from big business can only think *big*. They're thinking about scaling rather than thinking about creating good products for people. They're tempted to focus on the end point and think about the macro (building large departments and a scalable revenue engine) rather than thinking about the micro: people, customers, problems, and pain points. If you spent your own time and money directly engaging with your audience, listening to what they have to say, and forming the company's mission and moves with that feedback in mind, then you have the ability to overtake the big guns *very* quickly.

When the world was run by huge businesses with endless funding, they were the only game in town, and their way was the only way. But micro-brands like the one you're going to build are the next wave. In this wave, you have to think small first in order to think big.

It's Not All Clear Skies and Paydays

In my career, I've sold (and bought) both big businesses and small businesses. I've been a part of a lot of acquisitions through my students, too. I've seen pretty much every way the deal can go down, and I've been involved with businesses post-acquisition as well.

Selling your company means handing over a lot of control, and when you are handing over your baby, you want to ensure that it's being adopted into the right home.

Few buyers will treat your company (or your customers) with the same care that you did. Few owners will have the grit, energy, and passion that you brought into your business. I (sadly) know this from experience. I have felt the burning frustration of watching as the business that I re-homed was neglected by its new owner.

That's frustrating, to say the least. When some of your future wealth is tied up in future payments from acquirers, and you're not sure you'll see any of that wealth, you can lose a lot of sleep and start to experience regret. Ask me how I know (actually, don't—I'll start yelling).

I have also seen when an acquisition goes extremely well, and the new owner takes a $10 million business and turns it into a $50 million (or more) business. That, of course, is the dream. To put yourself into a position for that to happen, you must understand what selling your company really *means*. If you understand the landscape of possibilities, you know what you're in for, you won't be blindsided if things don't go the way you would have wanted them to, and you will be able to course-correct to ensure that you're on the right side of your company's history.

I've seen companies make obvious mistakes after they buy a business. The biggest mistake was to waste money trying to "professionalize" the business. When they bring in expensive executives touting old-school forms of marketing to "professionalize" the highly profitable, your fast-growing company can slow to a crawl. I've seen this happen more than once, with new ownership completely ignoring the process I'd been using to stack the deck and stoke my audience (the process you've learned in this book). The money that used to go toward building and engaging with the audience went instead to magazine ads and executive salaries. The money that used to go into product development went into paying a crazy salary for an old sales manager with zero hustle. I'm not saying either choice is *inherently* bad; depending on the company, they might be what are needed. But it reflects how vulnerable big, established, well-capitalized companies are to small, nimble companies that are using modern-day marketing. Big companies are not capable of playing the same game as small companies. Doing small things *well* is usually quite disruptive to what old, established businesses are often doing: a big thing *badly*.

That disruption is not something to which the big companies respond to gracefully. For example, in our third year at Sheer Strength, Matt and I sponsored a major bodybuilding show. When we got there, it turned out that our audience-focused online marketing was working gangbusters. We were the talk of the show. Attendees kept saying, "I see you guys everywhere! You're all over Amazon. You're all over Facebook." They all wanted to network with a company run by two scrawny Midwestern kids, who themselves were in awe of all the other huge sponsors at the show.

We made these snarky t-shirts that we handed out: *I bought some supplements on Amazon, and now I look like this.* They were a huge hit with everyone but the reps from the big companies. Things got a little confrontational. "It's people like you who are ruining the supplement industry by selling online instead of in retail stores" was a line we heard a lot.

That was evidence that our approach was working. We were beating the big guys at a game they weren't even equipped to play. Also, because those big companies weren't equipped to play the new game, we had a leg up on how our business was built. The majority of big businesses are totally left in the dust when it comes to targeting a specific audience and giving them what they want. They're just not agile enough to be able to do that.

Trying to bring a slow-moving big-business style of machine into a fast-moving industry like e-commerce usually involves wasting a lot of money. For instance, one of the acquirers I sold to only purchased my company as a leverage point for launching a bunch of other brands. They wanted to become the Procter & Gamble of Amazon. They bought my business as a case study of how to scale well, so that they could build a huge infrastructure aimed at replicating the style of business I'd built.

Initially, I was honored that they saw my company as the example they wanted to follow. It meant a lot to me, so much so that I stayed involved after the sale to advise them for a year. On our weekly calls, I'd tell them the exact same thing every time: "You're lost in scale and replication. You're thinking too big. You're not implementing any of the things that built this company in the first place."

They completely ignored me. They couldn't see it my way, because they could only think big. As a result, they lost millions of dollars in investments by trying to scale fast before having any specificity. I've seen this happen time and time again, not just with my own companies I've sold. I've seen acquisitions from older, rich businesspeople who are literally trying to buy the speed and momentum of internet businesses.

They're set up for failure right from the beginning. It's impossible to maintain the momentum of somebody who's thinking small if all you can do is think big.

What I learned from this is how effective the strategy in this book works, and how vulnerable big companies are. The minute that they lose connection with their customers, the faster they will go out of business. You hold the cards, not them.

When Should You Sell?

Once you hit a consistent 100 sales per day, the game changes. The years that follow will be spent growing that from $1 million to $3 million to $5 million per year. When you've crossed that initial million-dollar mark, you're in "The Gold," where you start to invest your profits into other areas of growth: new forms of advertising, new sponsorships, podcast advertising, content creation, scaling the logistics, and, most importantly, building teams to run it all. You'll be building the infrastructure to cultivate a real business out of what was formerly pretty much just a well-oiled sales machine.

It's only a business if you can walk away from it and it can successfully grow without you. If you're doing everything, if you're the integral cog in the machine without which everything crashes Jenga-style to the floor, then it's a sales machine, not a business. A business requires a higher level of hiring, systems, and optimizations. That's why my first hire when I hit the million-dollar mark was someone who enjoys organizing my chaos, so that I can keep thinking about growth. Hiring presents its own set of challenges, and your job at that stage will be to become the leader that your company needs to grow beyond you. That's often the point when you'll say, "I think I've grown this business to my greatest capacity as an entrepreneur. It's time to hand my baby over to someone who can grow it into a well-adjusted teenager."

At this point, your company stands on the brink of making a lot of mistakes. Avoid the following:

1. Optimizing for vanity metrics. It's very tempting to compare yourself (and your business) to things like your follower count, total number of sales (instead of profit), social media metrics, celebrity endorsements, or the size of your team. All these metrics boil down to is making you feel good about how many people like you—and they make you feel good when compared to a competitor. But they mean very little when it comes to the health and growth of your business. It's *very* tempting to place a high valuation on your business because of the number of fans or celebrity endorsements you can claim. But does this serve your customers? Does this equal real value or company health? I once watched one of my competitors build their entire business on buying Instagram followers and sponsoring hot Instagram models and bodybuilders. They had a crappy product, and they covered it up by pursuing short-term attention and authority. They eventually got torched. Vanity metrics make you feel good about yourself in the short term, but they don't create value for anything but your own ego.

2. Forgetting you're in the people business. Remember, this all comes back to people. You're not in the *product* business; you're in the *people* business. Launching products two, three, four, and five, and watching each one do well and snowball your revenue, is addicting. But don't let that lead you to simply throwing more and more products out there, chasing that high. It can divert your focus and set the precedent that your company is all about products first, customers second. You also run the risk that your customer will be equally distracted. As Moiz Ali told my attendees at one of our conferences, "When Native Deodorant got huge, there were a lot of people telling us we should do a toothpaste and a soap. But we were so focused on our one customer that we decided not to rush. We stayed in our lane."

3. Making decisions based on algorithms. I've often seen entrepreneurs fall into the habit of taking their cues from algorithms rather than people. For example, it's common for business owners to look at internal metrics and make product decisions based on what's already hot on Amazon. The temptation there is short-term cash and tapping opportunities just to bring in immediate dollars. It's not brand-building. It doesn't factor in the customer *at all*, and your business will suffer. It's like playing whack-a-mole: *Fill this inventory, sell this product. Fill this inventory, sell this product.* You might get fifty or more sales per day, but it won't compound your existing products, and your snowball will never build. Only invest in products and ideas that can have a multiplication effect on your business, and avoid the incremental short-term wins.

You Hold the Cards

One thing I wish I'd known going into acquisition is that if you've got a cool, popular, profitable business on your hands, you're the hot girl at the party. Everyone wants you. You're the one with the assets. You're the one with the negotiating power. The people wanting to buy your business don't have the power and control—you do.

If I had known that, it would have made the negotiation process so much different. I would have entered negotiations with my criteria and demands front and center. I would have told every interested party: "Here's what I'm looking for; can you meet these demands?" Most people selling their companies go into negotiations with exactly the opposite mindset: "What's the fastest route to my paycheck?" And whichever buyer produces that check fastest wins. Without realizing it, you're signing your life away for a short-term payout when you should be thinking about long-term goals—a contradiction of the long-term focus that got your business off the ground and scaled in the first place.

If I had known ahead of time that I needed to keep my long-term focus, I wouldn't have been blinded by the dollars I was about to receive and instead would have been more protective of my company. If I'd known what I know now going into my first acquisition, I would have been the one vetting the buying company, not the other way around. In multiple cases, after I sold a business and saw what was being done to it, I tried to buy it back. When I got on the phone with the new owners, I actually said to them, "The only reason I'm on the phone with you right now is because I gave my dog to a bad home and he's being abused and I need to rescue him."

Selling your company is not 100 percent transactional. It's not like selling a product. It's not a clean break. There will be a lot of emotion and expectation tied up in it. Done wrong, it can cause you much pain down the road and feel like a missed opportunity—or an opportunity that you had in your hands, and squandered.

When you sell your business, it's rare that you sell 100 percent of it and then walk away. Instead, it is more likely that you will sell a majority stake—usually about 60 percent—and hold onto the remaining portion. You will almost certainly serve as an advisor until the new owners are up to speed. Therefore, you must like the people that you are doing business with, and you must trust that they are capable of growing the business to the level that it can be.

That is why so much of my focus is working with entrepreneurs who have crossed seven figures and help them navigate the next stage of their business. I join them as a minority partner—usually 20 percent—and help them grow, get ready for sale, and ensure that the payday that they receive is the payday that they deserve.

What's It Like on the Other Side?

I have very publicly shared what it feels like to wake up and look at $10 million in my bank account. I have also shared that it didn't automatically mean my life was perfect (but you probably saw that coming).

In the weeks I was negotiating the close of the sale of my business, I was also going through a separation. In fact, when I came home from getting the check, all the furniture in my apartment was gone.

There I was, a multimillionaire, and all I had in my home was a pull-out couch that became a twin bed. I was so broke that all I had was money.

That is not to imply that the business had anything to do with my challenges at home. There's no neat narrative thread to tie this all up; there's no dramatic way to correlate the two. It was simply the case that I had one part of my life that was going great, and one part that was in shambles. On my Instagram, it was all celebration and wins; in real life, it was lonely. I used to think about how there were probably people out there comparing their lives unfavorably to mine based on my social media. We all walk around comparing ourselves to the tiny curated slices of life people put up on social media. It's not real.

Many people think money will fix all their problems—*nope*. It changes nothing but the size of your bank account. People go through incredible financial wins and deep financial losses, but it's not the point of life. It's an accomplishment, not what life is about.

Money gives you the fuel to build a great life. Part of the role of an entrepreneur is to define what that life is—to define how to live life on their own terms. Honestly—and I'm not being judgmental—most of us are pretty bad at that. We're all great at defining exactly how much money we want to make, or what we want our vanity metrics to be, how we want to stack up against others. We're not very good at defining what our actual experience of life is.

Once you've made a lot of money, you do one of two things. You can shrug and use the opportunity to do it again: *I guess I'll just start another business, and I'll figure out what it all means later.* Or you can do the hard self-discovery work of defining what you want your life to be about. One of the things I wish someone had told me back when I was a dreaming, ambitious, nineteen-year-old was to get intentional about what I wanted my life to look like once I had all the money I would ever need. Because money is like alcohol: it makes whatever is true come to the surface. If you give an insecure person a lot of money, they don't become more secure; they become more insecure. If you give a giving person a lot of money, they become more giving.

I wish that I had been challenged to cultivate a great life *before* I made a lot of money. Part of my journey after my first business was sold was uncovering what I thought a great life even looked like. I had no clue. I traded a lot of time and energy for money, and I got it—and then I found on the other side that it was just as much, or even *more*, work to cultivate a truly happy life.

Once you do have the money, you'll have the space and the cover you need to go deep and build an intentional life. I didn't do that. I made the mistake of putting it off even further. I started new businesses and initiatives and burned myself out due to my resistance to personal growth. In doing so, I discovered that the things I was resisting, or the things I overlooked, were actually what brought me happiness.

Happiness is found in your relationships, how you spend your time, and the small things that you enjoy. Money expands your menu of options. Some people use those options to deepen their relationships, deepen their enjoyment, and deepen their appreciation of the little things. Others stay blind to them, so they use money to buy new distractions and expand their own ego metrics. The person who does the former grows old, rich, and happy. The person who does the latter self-destructs.

If you choose to take on that personal work *while* your company is in its growth process, there's a great chance your company will be more profitable, will make you happier, and will support the overall life you want. Don't trade that potential for money. To paraphrase Benjamin Franklin, "Those who trade freedom for security deserve neither."

I'm not quite as judgmental as old Ben, but those words ring true. If you trade happiness for money, you'll end up losing both.

The Adventure Never Ends

It was December when Matt and I first got Sheer Strength to the million-dollar mark—almost six months to the day from when we took our first sale. I spent that winter, weirdly enough, in a bit of a funk. I mentioned this earlier when I told the story of my dinner with Tim Ferriss. I'd made a huge amount of money, and I'd inarguably smashed my childhood goal of becoming a millionaire, but I wasn't happy.

Okay, I made it to this big achievement. What do I do now? Am I done? Do I keep going? Do I start another business?

There's a weird almost-depression that happens when you reach the million-dollar mark. It's a whole new type of self-discovery. You wonder if you're really as good as you think you are; you wonder if you deserve it. Most of all, you wonder if it'll all go away at any moment.

It sounds crazy, but if there's a big pain point in the method I outline in this book, it's that it works almost *too* quickly. Your brain doesn't have a chance to catch up to the new level of success you're in, and it reacts by going into defense mode. You sit at your computer endlessly watching all the pieces of your business, trying to make sure no fires start. You've only allowed yourself to think right up to the edge of the million-dollar mark, and now that you're past it, you revert to playing whack-a-mole with (largely invented) emergencies.

My whole thought pattern at this time was in the groove of *if I stop moving, it'll all go away.* It was exhausting. A part of me was annoyed that I still hadn't made enough money to buy the Cleveland Indians, a life goal of mine since I could walk.

When I decided I was going to put on the Capitalism Conference, a conference for budding entrepreneurs featuring the best minds in business, I started out, like any total amateur, Googling speaking bureaus and cold-calling to try to land the people I wanted to speak. It took some persistence—and figuring out how to sound like I knew what I was doing *way* more than I actually did—but I managed to book Gary Vaynerchuk, of whom I'd been a fan since 2008, way before *#AskGaryVee* or VaynerMedia. The second person I booked was Robert Herjavec, from *Shark Tank*, because I'd seen the impact a physical products brand had on the show. The third person I booked was Grant Cardone, and at the time I thought there was a lot I could learn from him. (Nope.) I've publicly documented my beef with Grant on the podcast, but let's just say that when you meet your heroes, you sometimes run the risk of realizing that you don't want to be anything like them.

I ran the first CapCon simply as a way to elevate my thinking and my knowledge, and do the same for my friends and the dedicated band of followers I'd gained sharing my business-building on my YouTube channel and podcast. I did it because, after reaching the million-dollar mark, I needed to see what the next steps looked like. I figured that I could crowdsource the path by bringing together as many uber-successful entrepreneurs as my budget would allow.

It was a huge success—enough to immediately plan year two—but after that conference, I had the same little comedown I'd had after my business made it to seven figures. The same thing happened! I was mildly depressed and unsure of what to do next. *Now what?*

A friend of mine, Todd Herman, called me up after the event and asked how I was feeling. I was honest with him about the funk I was in.

"You know why, right?" he asked.

"No. Why?"

"Because you planned up to the goal, but not *through* the goal."

He explained that it's common to get depressed after you hit a goal because you don't know what's next. If you plan *through* the goal, though, the goal itself is just another step on a longer journey.

He was right. After a couple years of CapCon, I started to see deep correlations between the people I brought onstage to talk and my own journey. I started to expand my perspective of what was possible. My lens widened. I started to see myself not just as a successful entrepreneur but as a mentor; I wanted to help other people achieve their own business dreams by sharing the path through the jungle I'd hacked out with grit, guesswork, and, honestly, a shitload of stubbornness.

And there had been one more *very* important factor in my success. Through it all, I'd had incredible mentors.

We can all point to moments in our life that changed everything. I hope that reading this book becomes one of those moments for you. One of those life-defining moments happened when I accidentally sneaked into a bar to meet Travis Sago, who would later become my long-standing mentor. That ultimately paved the way for my success, and ultimately to the writing of this book. When you hit your first million, you will have this accidental barhop to thank.

When I was nineteen, I was, believe it or not, attending ministry school. I was studying to be a pastor. Remember when I told you that starting down this path was opening Pandora's box, and you wouldn't recognize yourself at the other end? *Case in point.*

Deep down, I knew that I was attending ministry school out of guilt, and that what I really wanted was to be an entrepreneur. I'd never lost that spark that had started that day I asked my dad how much a million dollars was and decided I'd become a millionaire. I'd been carefully guarding and kindling that flame all along—constant little hustles throughout high school, running a scrappy dorm-room internet marketing business while preparing for a career in the church—and the vast gulf between what I was *planning* and what I *wanted* was starting to wear me down.

That's what led me to take a few days off and fly to San Diego to attend a conference for internet entrepreneurs. I was making a full-time income from my college dorm room, and that's hot shit when you're bragging to your buddies, but I knew that I was just "guessing" at it. If I was going to be a true entrepreneur, then I needed help building a real business. I needed someone to guide me. I told my mom that I was going to the conference to learn how to grow my business, but I went for one reason: to meet Travis.

I walked into the bar that evening thinking that it was only a restaurant; a few hours later, when it turned into a dance club, I had no idea what was going on. (Life hack: It's not technically sneaking into a bar underage if you go there for dinner and then stay out of sight until after they start checking IDs.) I was distinctly the youngest person there. I didn't drink at all, and I *still* don't know how to talk to girls. Talk about being out of my element.

Travis went by "BumMarketer" on the internet forum where we met. Don't let that fool you—even in our digital conversations, I could tell that this was a person who could teach me everything I craved learning. I figured that if I could get Travis to meet me and remember me, then it would be worth it. After all, no one was showing me how to play this game. Entrepreneurship is lonely on its own, but when you grow up without a mentor—spending most of your days alone, trying not to binge the peanut butter because you are depressed about your parents divorcing— you deeply crave the guidance of someone to show you the way.

And that night in San Diego, sitting in the dark, watching girls dance on the dance floor and drinking a tall glass of water, I prayed that fate would find me. Because when someone like me—and like you—has the chance to meet someone who can cut the learning curve, I'll move heaven and earth to meet them. For me, that person was Travis. I believed that he could help illuminate the path for me.

This was my chance.

I was mid-conversation with a couple of dudes who I knew from the internet business world ("internet marketing" was still kind of a niche thing back then) when I saw Travis walk in. I left the conversation mid-sentence to go introduce myself.

Nervous as hell, I said, "Hey, Travis, I'm Ryan."

Travis got a huge smile on his face, and I found myself enveloped in a huge Arkansas-country-boy hug. "Oh hey! Ryan!"

Apparently, he recognized me from the internet. That felt good.

"What are you drinking, Ryan?"

I didn't know how to answer. I didn't drink. In fact, I had signed a contract at my college vowing not to drink alcohol or participate in any sexual activity until after I graduated. I was also not allowed to participate in "social dancing." Probably because it led to drinking. Or maybe I couldn't have sex because it led to dancing. I'm not sure. I still don't quite get the order.

Anyway, I think I asked Travis for a Coke or a water, while he ordered a scotch. Years later, he would turn me into a scotch drinker. If you ever run into me in person and feel like buying me a drink, I'll take a Glenlivet 15. But *only* one. I start slurring words after two.

I remember that Travis invited me outside to sit on the patio, and we talked until I literally couldn't keep my eyes open anymore. And I remember walking back to my hotel, wondering if I'd ever see him again.

Either way, I was confident that I had accomplished one of my goals: Travis knew who I was, and he would, with hope, remember my name. I knew that finding the right mentor could be a five-to-ten-year process. (In fact, as I write this, I'm boarding a flight to meet with a mentor that I have been courting for two years.) I felt like that night at the bar I might have just cut the line a little. I knew that I would be an entrepreneur for life, and I was only in the warmup process. A mentor could change everything for me.

The next morning, I stumbled from my hotel room to the conference, exhausted but still buzzing from the night before. I waited in a long registration line to check in at the conference. I had no idea what to expect there; I was only hoping that I would meet some people who could help open opportunities for me. While I awkwardly stood in line among entrepreneurs twice my age (and probably ten times as successful as me), I felt a tap on my shoulder.

"Hey, dude!"

I turned, and there was Travis's friendly face again, fresh-eyed and somehow far more awake than me.

He remembered me. This was a good sign.

"I want you to meet someone," he said. Travis pointed to some kid who was rounding the corner. We met glances and froze. We were definitely the only kids under twenty-one there.

Travis said, "You guys are probably the youngest people here. You should talk. See ya later!"

And he was off to the next conversation. In that brief interaction, though, he'd changed the course of my entire life, because the random kid he'd pointed out to me? That was Matt.

I think back on that moment all the time. Travis barely knew me; what did he have to gain from staying up all night to talk to me or make a life-changing introduction (not that either of us knew that at the time)? He was *far more* valuable to me than I was to him.

But that's the point: Travis wasn't in it for the value he could *get*. He was in it for the value he could *create*. He saw what I had inside: the deep conviction that entrepreneurship was the passion I was willing to sacrifice for, and that I might be a good horse to bet on.

I don't remember anything else from that conference. All I remember is that I met two people: Matt and Travis. Travis would become my mentor for the next decade—although he says that we're more like brothers at this point. Matt would become a good friend and, five years later, my business partner. He would be right there with me as we developed, tested, and proved the method I taught you in this book.

From the day we met, Matt and I shared that deep, dedicated drive to be successful. Through five years of ups, downs, wins, losses, successes, and failures, we kept trying. I've heard people say that the definition of insanity is doing the same thing over and over, expecting a different result; to me, that's just the definition of an entrepreneur. The only way you can go from hustler to entrepreneur is by going all in. And if you're having trouble making that choice, maybe you need a swift kick. Matt and I each got a big one that ended up pushing us all in. After five years, we were close to giving up on building anything "real." Then our motivation arrived, one by one, in the form of two plus signs.

My plus sign arrived on my twenty-sixth birthday, more than half a decade after the conference where I'd met Matt and Travis. It was my birthday, and my girlfriend and I had tickets to the Austin City Limits music festival. We had a big breakfast at Kerbey Lane Cafe and then went back to her apartment to change.

"I'm a day late," she casually said. "Just let me pee on this stick so I can drink with a clear conscience."

Long story short, we didn't go to the music festival. Instead, we held each other, crying—sometimes excited and sometimes scared as hell—as we mentally wrapped our heads around the fact that we were pregnant.

My first call was to Matt. "Dude, I'm gonna be a dad. We need to figure our shit out."

There was no doubt: I was *all in*. I had no choice but to make our business work.

My second phone call was to Travis. He had become more than a business mentor by then. After years of help navigating business challenges, Travis had also taught me about life, leadership, and being a man. He calmed me down, helped me get my bearings, and picked me up when I was crumbling. I was about to go on two adventures: learning how to be an entrepreneur, and learning how to be a dad.

A few months later, after moving into a house with a bunch of baby furniture, ready to start my new adventure, my phone rang. It was Matt. Our business was starting to show some signs of life, and I thought that he was calling me to give me the updated sales numbers. Nope! He called to tell me something else entirely.

"Ryan," Matt said, "is there such thing as a false positive pregnancy test?" (I dare you to think of a better way to start a phone call.)

I guess serendipity brought Matt and me together twice; this time, it was in the form of two very random pregnancy tests. We were both all in. We had the drive. We had the mindset. We had the passion. We had the idea. But this kicked us both into gear. Together we built a million-dollar business.

With this book in your hands, reader, you have everything you need to do the same. This method *will work*. But will you? Or do you need your own plus sign (proverbial, of course) to kick you into action?

For the next twelve months, you're going to be focused on the steps outlined in this book. You're going to realize your dream of freedom through entrepreneurship. Here at the end of the book I want to make sure you understand that twelve months to a million is just the first twelve months on a much longer journey. If you are like most entrepreneurs, the business will only be half the journey. This adventure will show you who you are, and it will force you to become more. It will force you to take more responsibility, it will humble you to your knees at times, and it will teach you what is important in life. Entrepreneurship is a beautiful portal into self-discovery.

There will be times that you get frustrated and want to quit. There will be many times when you wonder, *What is this all for?* And there will be times of incomparable excitement. Keep going through all of it. As Steve Jobs famously said, *You can only connect the dots backwards.* Success is never a linear path. It's filled with ins and outs, ups and downs, and weird left turns. Ultimately, who you become along the way is what is most interesting. When you become the kind of person who is responsible, happy, and giving, that's when you are unstoppable. That is also when you get rich.

The tagline for Capitalism.com is to "Create Change," because it takes just one person to go all in. It not only changes your financial future but can also change an industry. It can change *your* world, if not *the world.*

Life will keep giving you the opportunity to learn, to grow, and to expand, and these developments will be reflected in your business. As I write this, I've been outlining my next business, and I'm confident it will be more successful than all the previous ones combined. Shortly after signing the papers, I learned that my second child is on the way.

I am, once again, *all in.*

I am all in *for you*, too.

INDEX